DIESTERWEGS

NEUSPRACHLICHE

BIBLIOTHEK

The Many Voices of English

An Anthology of Post-Colonial Short Stories

Teacher's Book

by Angelika Hoff, Stefanie Münzner and Tom Whalen

D1728972

DIESTERWEG

The Many Voices of English
An Anthology of Post-Colonial Short Stories

Teacher's Book
by Angelika Hoff, Stefanie Münzner and Tom Whalen

© 2006 Bildungshaus Schulbuchverlage
Westermann Schroedel Diesterweg
Schöningh Winklers GmbH, Braunschweig
www.diesterweg.de

Druck A [1] / Jahr 2006
Alle Drucke der Serie A sind im Unterricht parallel verwendbar.

Redaktion: Angelika Hoff, Korntal
Herstellung und Layout: Harald Thumser, Frankfurt
Satz: Satzpunkt Ewert GmbH, Bayreuth
Druck und Bindung: westermann druck GmbH, Braunschweig

ISBN 978-3-425-**09031**-3
    alt: 3-425-**09031**-3

Table of Contents

The dates indicate when the short stories were first published.

Preface

This teaching guide has been designed to supplement Rudolph F. Rau's annotations as an aid for your lessons on the eleven stories collected in *The Many Voices of English*.

In order to help you meet some of the pedagogical challenges the stories present, the chapters are broken into two principle parts: Interpretation and Teaching Suggestions. In the former, you will find a summary of the story, bringing into relief some of its significant elements, followed by a close look at a few formal aspects and thematic concerns. A section entitled "Background Information" deals with a related topic, sometimes formal, sometimes thematic, sometimes extra-contextual (e.g., the elements of plot; folk tale vs. modern short story; an overview of Rushdie's controversial novel *The Satanic Verses*; a history of black Madonnas). Under "Teaching Suggestions" we have included activities for pre-, while-, and after-reading of the story, as well as questions and topics for class discussion or composition. Creative activities and topics for student presentations are also included.

Each story in *The Many Voices of English*, no matter its level of artistry and thematic complexity, presents its own interpretative difficulties, in large part due to the issues that swirl up and around (not unlike a Conradian fog) the ideological country, so to speak, of post-colonialism. May the material you encounter in this guide help you navigate the terrain.

– Tom Whalen (4 August 2006)

Joseph Conrad
"An Outpost of Progress" (1896)

Interpretation and Background Information

Joseph Conrad's "An Outpost of Progress"

As with other important works by Conrad such as *Heart of Darkness* (1899) and *Victory* (1910), this richly textured tale is a critique of colonialism and its so-called civilizing influence on "the dark continent". Vivid description and characterization, within the framework of an adventure story (strangers in a strange land), are set beside ironic commentary and Conrad's attempt to probe the metaphysics of the matter.

Summary of "An Outpost of Progress"

Two Belgians, Kayerts and Carlier, both failures in their careers back home, are put in charge of a trading station in the Belgian Congo, when the colony was ruled by the rapacious policies of King Leopold II. But it's the "third man on the staff" who is really in charge, "a Sierra Leone nigger" who calls himself Henry Price but is more widely known in the area as Makola. Married to a "negress from Loanda," Makola, having worked with the previous station chief who died of a fever (he's buried "under a tall cross much out of the perpendicular" (p. 12)), is the one who knows the business, the region and its people.

After the director of the Great Trading Company, "a man ruthless and efficient, who at times, but very imperceptibly, indulged in grim humour" (pp. 14–15), delivers supplies, a disingenuous speech, and the promise to return in six months, he tells an old employee of the company that he "always thought the station on this river useless, and they [Kayerts and Carlier] fit the station!", to which the old employee replies that Kayerts and Carlier "will form themselves there" (p. 16). The formation of their characters is what the story depicts and, as it soon becomes clear, will be more a *deformation*.

When they're "left unassisted to face the wilderness" (p. 16), our "two perfectly insignificant and incapable individuals" huddle together "as children do in the dark" (p. 17). In their naiveté Kayerts and Carlier remain in the dark. They laugh together, plan their days, think less of one another than they say, and glide along for a while on their optimism, unaware that "society" has made them, "through want of practice, incapable of independent thought" (p. 20). Soon both of them "regretted" their previous lives, Kayerts "his post in the Administration of the Telegraph" (if it weren't that his daughter Melie needed a dowry, he thinks, he wouldn't stay in the Congo), Carlier "the clink of sabre and spurs on a fine afternoon" (p. 21) – he had been a non-commissioned officer in the cavalry.

They idle their days away and let Makola run the station, living instead "like blind men in a large room, aware only of what came in contact with them (and that only imperfectly), but unable to see the general aspect of things. The river, the forest, all the great emptiness. Even the brilliant sunshine disclosed nothing intelligible" (p. 21). They mock the natives, they swagger about, "understanding nothing" (p. 22) of their surroundings or of themselves. "Here, look! look at that fellow there – and that other one, to the left. Did you ever [see] such a face? Oh, the funny brute!" "Pah! Don't they stink!" (p. 22) After a few months our "two pioneers of trade and progress" have begun to curse "this dog of a country! " (p. 23)

"The two men understood nothing, cared for nothing but for the passage of days that separated them from the steamer's return" (p. 24). They read – naively, sentimentally, poorly – "wrecks of novels" left in tatters by their predecessor. They read an article called "Our Colonial Expansion" from an old copy of their home paper. One day "Carlier went and replanted the cross firmly. [...] 'And solid, I promise you! I suspended myself with both hands to the cross-piece. Not a move. Oh, I did that properly.'" (p. 25)

Sometimes they're visited by "the chief of the neighbouring villages" Gobila, "a gray-headed savage, thin and black, with a white cloth round his loins and a mangy panther skin hanging over his back" (pp. 25–26). They take "a liking for that old and incomprehensible creature, and called him Father Gobila" (p. 26), though they cannot understand what he says to them. Because of Gobila's respect and reverence for the two white men, his village supplies them with food, though Gayerts and Carlier still suffer bouts of fever that leave them "weaker, and their appearance changed for the worse" (p. 27).

"Five months passed in that way," summarizes Conrad in a one-sentence paragraph a third of the way through his tale (p. 27).

The first major turn occurs when armed Loandan traders from the coast arrive at the station. "They were tall, slight, draped classically from neck to heel in blue fringed cloths, and carried percussion muskets over their bare right shoulders." (Muskets, of course, courtesy of the colonial powers.) Their speech is "like a reminiscence of something not exactly familiar, and yet resembling the speech of civilized men. It sounded like one of those impossible languages which sometimes we hear in our dreams" (p. 28). An amalgam of African, colonialist, and "dream" mystification – "they [...] strolled about with an air of ease, put their heads through the door of the storeroom, congregated round the grave, pointed understandingly at the cross, and generally made themselves at home" (p. 29) – these traders even Makola fears. Since he cannot understand their language, his wife has to intercede as the interpreter. Unbeknownst to Kayerts and Carlier, an exchange is negotiated: six large elephant tusks for the Company's ten indentured slaves, "a warlike tribe with filed teeth" from the interior (p. 32), grown sick and weak, in body and spirit.

The presence of the intruders from the coast produces for our unheroic strangers in a dark and mysterious land the following insight: "They both, for the first time, became aware that they lived in conditions where the unusual may be dangerous, and that there was no power on earth outside of themselves to stand between them and the unusual" (p. 29). "All night," we're told, Kayerts and Carlier "were disturbed by a lot of drumming in the villages [...] as if the whole land had been one immense drum booming out steadily an appeal to heaven. And through the deep and tremendous noise sudden yells that resembled snatches of songs from a madhouse darted shrill and high in discordant jets of sound which seemed to rush far above the earth and drive all peace from under the stars" (pp. 30–31).

The next day Makola receives their permission to negotiate a trade for ivory. "'Bad fellows,' said Makola, indifferently. 'They fight with people, and catch women and children. They are bad men, and got guns. There is a great disturbance in the country. Do you want ivory?'" The answer is immediate: "Yes" (p. 33).

Makola refrains from telling Kayerts directly that he plans on trading their "no-good" workmen, though a wiser man than Kayerts would have understood. That night, "Carlier waking suddenly, heard a man shout loudly; then a shot was fired." When he and Kayerts investigate, Makola shoos them back in their house, telling them to "Say nothing! I know my business" (p. 34). They don't discover until morning that Makola has sold the men from the interior and that one of Gobila's villagers has been killed.

Initially Kayerts and Carlier express moral outrage that their men have been sold for ivory – "You fiend! [...] I dismiss you! I will report you – I won't look at the tusk." (p. 36–37) – and to one another agree that "Slavery is an awful thing" (p. 36). "They believed their words," Conrad's third person omniscient narrator says. "Everybody shows a respectful deference to certain sounds that he and his fellows can make. [...] Nobody knows what suffering or sacrifice mean – except, perhaps, the victims of the mysterious purpose of these illusions" (38-39). The next morning they help Makola weigh and store the ivory. Carlier reasons: "It's deplorable, but, the men being Company's men the ivory is Company's ivory. We must look after it" (p. 40).

Having participated in the violation of one of civilization's moral imperatives, the deformation of the two Belgians proceeds apace. "It was not the absolute and dumb solitude of the post that impressed them so much as an inarticulate feeling that something from within them was gone, something that worked for their safety, and had kept the wilderness from interfering with their hearts" (p. 41). In addition, Gobila, realizing now that "the witchcraft of white men [...] had brought wicked people into" his country, decides that the villagers "must keep away from them" (p. 41) and stops supplying the station with food. "In his fear, the mild old Gobila offered extra human sacrifices to all the Evil Spirits that had taken possession of his white friends. [...] Who could foresee the woe those mysterious creatures, if irritated, might bring?" (pp. 40–41)

For Kayerts and Carlier, living now on saltless rice and sugarless coffee, "the great silence of the surrounding wilderness, its very hopelessness and savagery seemed to approach them nearer, to draw them gently, to look upon them, to envelop them with a solicitude irresistible, familiar, and disgusting" (p. 41). As they wait for the steamer to arrive (it's two months late), Carlier begins to talk of "the necessity of exterminating all the niggers before the country be made habitable", and Kayerts spends "hours looking at the portrait of Melie" (p. 42). And they get sicker and sicker, weaker and weaker, while – in the meantime, a great distance away, as in a cinematic cutaway – "the Director of the Company "thought that the useless station, and the useless men, could wait" (p. 43).

Physically and morally degraded, the two of them descend to the level of the absurd, when Carlier demands Kayerts give him one of the fifteen remaining lumps of sugar for his coffee. Kayerts refuses, wanting to save them "in case of sickness" (both are already sick), which causes Carlier to call him a "stingy old slave-dealer" (p. 44). As if this were the worst insult he could receive, Kayerts replies, "That joke is in very bad taste. Don't repeat it." But Carlier does: "You are a slave-dealer. I am a slave-dealer. There's nothing but slave-dealers in this cursed country" (p. 45). Kayerts locks himself in his room with his gun and escapes outside when he hears Carlier try to break the door down. A bit of slapstick horror follows, as they chase one another around the house, until Kayerts, weak with fever, collapses in exhaustion. "He felt he could not, would not move any more. He was completely distracted by the sudden perception that the position was without issue – that death and life had in a moment become equally difficult and terrible" (p. 47).

But then he hears Carlier move, and as he "darted to the left, grasping his revolver, [...] at the very same instant, as it seemed to him, they came into violent collision. [...] A loud explosion took place between them; a roar of red fire" (p. 48). Thinking he's been shot, Kayerts expects he's about to die, but: "He did not die. Only his shoulder felt as if it had been badly wrenched, and he had lost his revolver. He was disarmed and helpless! He waited for his fate" (p. 48). Kayerts's death must wait, however. He "turned the corner [...] and nearly swooned. He had seen on the floor, protruding past the other corner, a pair of turned-up feet. A pair of white naked feet in red slippers" (pp. 48-49). Kayerts has killed Carlier. When Makola discovers that Carlier had no gun, Kayerts "found life more terrible and difficult than death. He had shot an unarmed man." Carlier "lay there with his right eye blown out" (p. 49).

After Makala suggests they say Carlier "died of a fever" (p. 49), Kayerts spends a hellish night with his dark thoughts: "He had plumbed in one short afternoon the depths of horror and despair, and now found repose in the conviction that life had no more secrets for him: neither had death!" He believes, "with that kind of wrong-headed lucidity which may be observed in some lunatics," that he has seen the truth. "He was at peace; he was familiar with the highest wisdom!" (p. 50) The next morning, delirious, he walks out into a "mist white and deadly, immaculate and poisonous" (p. 51), and hears a "shriek inhuman". It's the Company's steamer "like the yells of some exasperated and ruthless creature" piercing the silence. "Progress and civilization and all the virtues. Society was calling to its accomplished child to come, to be taken care of, to be instructed, to be judged, to be condemned; it called him to return to that rubbish heap from which he had wandered away, so that justice could be done." Kayerts "looked round like a man who has lost his way; and he saw a dark smudge, a cross-shaped stain, upon the shifting purity of the mist" (p. 52).

Upon this cross, the "Managing Director of the Great Civilizing Company (since we know that civilization follows trade)" (p. 53) finds Kayerts "hanging by a leather strap [...] He had evidently climbed the grave, which was high and narrow, and after tying the end of the strap to the arm, had swung himself off. His toes were only a couple of inches above the ground; his arms hung stiffly down; he seemed to be standing rigidly at attention, but with one purple cheek playfully posed on the shoulder. And, irreverently, he was putting out a swollen tongue at his Managing Director" (p. 54).

Narrative Structure and Parallelism

Conrad frames his volatile material with the appearances of the Managing Director at the beginning and end. Within this frame we observe the disintegration of Kayerts and Carlier. The conflict of the two with their new environment is established immediately and, along with their ignorance and their racist assumptions, propels the story's rising action – their increasing lethargy, sickness, and inability to meet their and the station's needs. At the crucial mid-point of the story the Loandan traders arrive and the reader learns (though not the two Belgians, not yet) that Makola will trade the stations workers for ivory. "There were ten station men who had been left by the Director. Those fellows, having engaged themselves to the Company for six months (without having any idea of a month in particular and only a very faint notion of time in general), had been serving the cause of progress for upwards of two years" (p. 31). The trading of the station men leads us to the story's climax (not to be confused with the story's climactic ending) two-thirds of the way into the tale, when they overcome their ethical scruples and help Makola with the ivory (p. 40). This change serves as the story's peripety that leads to the falling action and the two Belgians' continuing slide to their deaths. For the denouement, Conrad cuts away from Kayerts on his way to hang himself from the cross to the Managing Director. The framing device neatly closes the story, but the irony inherent in the picture of the dead Kayerts with his tongue sticking out at the Director (and us) deepens and spreads.

In addition to the framing device of the Director's departure and arrival, parallelism is used to juxtapose the so-called civilized and barbaric societies. The two Belgians do not understand Gobila, whom they see as an "old and incomprehensible creature" ("There he [Gobila] sat, watching Kayerts, and now and then making a speech which the other did not understand" (p. 26).) anymore than Gobila, to whom all whites were "indistinguishably alike" (p. 26), understands them ("Who could foresee the woe those mysterious creatures, if irritated, might bring?" (p. 41) The ten tribesmen from the interior who are sold as slaves to the armed Loandans, like Kayerts and Carlier, are a long way from home. Carlier, "like Kayerts, *regretted* his old life" (my emphasis p. 21); the tribesmen also "were not happy, *regretting* the festive incantations, the sorceries, the human sacrifices of their own land; where they also had parents, brothers, sisters, admired chiefs, respected magicians, loved friends, and other ties supposed generally to be human" (my emphasis; p. 32). We're told that the tribesmen do not believe in suicide ("Had they been of any other tribe they would have made up their minds to die – for nothing is easier to certain savages than suicide – and so have escaped from the puzzling difficulties of existence" (p. 32); Kayerts, on the other hand, is the "savage" who in the end is reduced to just such an expediency.

Other parallels are used for more purely ironic and symbolic effect. "My head is split," says Kayerts (p. 23), though it is he who will *split* Carlier's head when he accidentally shoots him through the eye. Our first view of Kayerts and Carlier, the one "short and fat", the other "tall, with [...] a long pair of thin legs" (p. 12) are comic types familiar to us in figures like Oliver Hardy and Stan Laurel (Dick und Doof) or Vladimir and Estragon from Beckett's *Waiting for Godot*. Appropriately, then, Kayerts and Carlier perform a comedy routine at the end as they chase one another around the house. And then there's the cross Carlier makes firm ("solid, I promise you! I suspended myself with both hands to the cross-piece" (p. 25)) and Kayerts hangs himself from.

Language: Description and Irony

In his preface to his novel *The Nigger of the "Narcissus"* (1897), Conrad stated that the literary artist's goal is "to make you hear, to make you feel ... before all, to make you see." "An Outpost of Progress" supplies ample evidence of his aesthetic. The Company's steamer "resembled an enormous sardine box with a flat-roofed shed erected on it" (p. 14). The natives "with spears in their hands [...] were naked, glossy black, ornamented with snowy shells and glistening brass wire, perfect of limb" (p. 21). When Kayerts comes upon Carlier after he's accidentally shot him, he sees "a pair of turned-up feet. A pair of white naked feet in red slippers" (p. 49).

But in order to make us *see* and *feel* the mystery and horror in the confrontation with the Other, Conrad also relies on abstractions like *mystery* and *horror*. The world around the station is "like a great emptiness" (p. 21). The river "flowed through a void" (p. 21). The wilderness is "rendered more strange, more incomprehensible by the mysterious glimpses of the vigorous life it contained" (pp. 16-17). Gobila believes the previous chief of the station "got himself buried for some mysterious purpose of his own" (p. 26); he can't "clear up that mystery" (p. 27). When Carlier and Kayerts make "certain sounds" (p. 38) against slavery, Conrad writes, "Nobody knows what suffering or sacrifice mean – except, perhaps the victims of the mysterious purpose of these illusions" (p. 39).

Often Conrad's style mixes concrete description with abstract rumination. As Kayerts and Carlier idle their days away letting Makola run the station, Conrad describes them as living "like blind men in a large room, aware only of what came in contact with them (and that only imperfectly), but unable to see the general aspect of things. The river, the forest, all the great emptiness. Even the brilliant sunshine disclosed nothing intelligible. Things appeared and disappeared before their eyes in an unconnected and aimless kind of way. The river seemed to come from nowhere and flow nowhither. It flowed through a void. Out of that void, at times, came canoes, and men with spears in their hands ..." (p. 21). This passage about the blindness of the station's new chief and his assistant is a good example of how Conrad fuses the concrete to the abstract in order to achieve a vision both psychologically true to the characters (their ignorance of their surroundings) and metaphysically compelling ("Even the brilliant sunshine disclosed nothing intelligible"). At the end of the passage, the abstractions that have threatened to overwhelm the description ("great emptiness", "nowhere", "void") returns to the concrete image of "men with spears in their hands".

In the following descriptive passage, by focusing exclusively on the aural, Conrad's prose takes on aspects of the grotesque and mad, like the shrill songs from the figurative madhouse reflected from within it.

> All night they were disturbed by a lot of drumming in the villages. A deep, rapid roll nearby would be followed by another far off – then all ceased. Soon short appeals would rattle out here and there, then all mingle together, increase, become vigorous and sustained, would spread out over the forest, roll through the night, unbroken and ceaseless, near and far, as if the whole land had been one immense drum booming out steadily an appeal to heaven. And through the deep and tremendous noise sudden yells that resembled snatches of songs from a madhouse darted shrill and high in discordant jets of sound which seemed to rush far above the earth and drive all peace from under the stars. (pp. 30-31)

Sound upon sound upon sound, booming an appeal to heaven, but producing instead only madhouse music that rushes and jets up, driving away "all peace from under the stars". Whatever the message, Conrad's insistent use of the sense of sound evokes the terror of the unknown.

Another notable feature of Conrad's style in "An Outpost of Progress" is the commentary of the omniscient narrator. (In subsequent works (*Heart of Darkness*, 1899; *Lord Jim*, 1900), he uses the mediating presence of his character Marlow to narrate his story to an auctorial "I" which somewhat leavens the outbursts of irony.) There are numerous instances of commentary in the story, e.g., "The courage, the composure, the confidence; the emotions and principles; every great and every insignificant thought belongs not to the individual but to the crowd: to the crowd that believes blindly in the irresistible force of its institutions and of its morals, in the power of its police and of its opinion" (p. 17).

More often the commentary is tinged with a hard, scathing irony: "Society, not from any tenderness, but because of its strange needs, had taken care of those two men, forbidding them all independent thought, all initiative, all departure from routine; and forbidding it under pain of death. They could only live on condition of being machines" (p. 19). Toward the end of the story, Conrad writes: "Progress was calling to Kayerts from the river. Progress and civilization and all the virtues. Society was calling to its accomplished child to come, to be taken care of, to be instructed, to be judged, to be condemned; it called him to return to that rubbish heap from which he had wandered away, so that justice could be done" (p. 52), and the Great Trading Company becomes the "Great Civilizing Company (since we know that civilization follows trade)" (p. 53).

The irony in the story, as in the ironic use of the word "progress" throughout and the story's final image, is, of course, more than a stylistic device. It reflects Conrad's own conflicted attitudes toward civilization and the *mystery* of mankind and morality. Conrad's "troublesome combination of pessimism and ambiguity," the critic Jakob Lothe notes in his essay on "An Outpost of Progress" ("Conrad's Fiction as Narrative Concentration" in *Joseph Conrad: Critical Assessments*, 1992), "is enhanced through the diverse use of irony. The range of irony is remarkable: it moves beyond the commentary of the story's authorial theorizing intellect, it is more sophisticated and varied; and in this capacity it modifies the authority of the authorial narrator while at the same time increasing the short story's overall complexity and suggestiveness."

Characterization and the Effects of Colonialism

The threshold where civilization meets the primitive is, one would think, ripe for cross-cultural exchange, and in a sense, a rather perverted one in "An Outpost of Progress", this proves to be the case. In order to better understand the effects of the colonial collision at work in the story, we can break its characters down to three divisions – the Africans (Makola, his wife, Gobila), the two African groups (ten station men from the interior; traders from Loanda), and the Belgians (Director, Kayerts, Carlier) – and observe that, at least within this tale, colonialism offers nothing of positive value. As it turns out, the collision of Kayerts and Carlier that leads to both of their deaths – one by accident, the other suicide – is the outcome of the larger cultural collision the story rests on.

I. The Africans

Makola, the "Sierra Leone nigger" who says his name is Henry Price, is the representative figure of this cultural exchange. Trained by the colonialists, he can speak several native tongues as well as English and French, and keeps the books for the Company station. It is he who understands best the Company's business and desires and is willing to sell the station workers into slavery for tusks of ivory. "I did the best for you and the Company," he tells his two superiors. "Why you shout so much? Look at this tusk" (p. 36). Adapting the ways of the Company, he's the one who offers the cover-up for Carlier's death by proposing fever as the cause.

Makola's wife, "a negress from Loanda, very large and very noisy" (p. 12) with three children and one on the way, at first seems an isolated figure. She, too, is not from the Congo and doesn't interact with the Belgians. Instead, however, when the Loandan armed traders appear, since she's from the same region, she serves as the interpreter and mediator in the exchange. Without her presence, it's likely that the station would have been sacked and its workers either captured or killed. In themselves, she and her husband represent an inter-African cultural exchange.

For Gobila, "the chief of the neighbouring villages" (p. 25), white men "all appeared [...] very young, indistinguishably alike (except for stature), and he knew that they were all brothers, and also immortal. The death of the artist [the first station chief, dead from a fever], who was the first white man whom he knew intimately, did not disturb this belief, because he was firmly convinced that the white stranger had pretended to die and got himself buried for some mysterious purpose of his own, into which it was useless to inquire. Perhaps it was his way of going home to his own country? At any rate, these were his brothers, and he transferred his absurd affection to them" (p. 26). The unknown produces a sense of awe and reverence in him – characteristic of primitive societies, one might say, until we begin to examine so-called civilization's fantastic and utterly unfounded beliefs. What is incomprehensible for Gobila becomes a site for awe and fear. In the confrontation with the Other, one tendency is simply not to see the Other, or at least not as what she or he really is. For Gobila, all white people look alike. When one of the villagers is killed by the Loandans, Gobila rightly reasons that it was due to the white man's influence, and he then decides to sever his ties to them, though he is no less in awe or fear of them. Gobila's willingness to see the Belgians as his "brothers", as it turns out for at least one of his tribe, was a grave doctrinal error.

II. The Two African Groups

Conrad goes out of his way to point to the connection between the traders from Loanda and the West. Their speech resembles "the speech of civilized men. It sounded like one of those impossible languages which sometimes we hear in our dreams" (p. 28). Though "draped classically from neck to heel in blue fringed cloths" (note, however, the "civilized" adverb *classically*), they carry "percussion muskets" (p. 28) which could only have been obtained by trade with the colonialists. They are also, we see when they enter the compound, familiar with the dominant religious myth of the West, Christianity: they "pointed understandingly at the cross, and generally made themselves at home" (p. 29).

From the interior, the darkest, so to speak, part of the dark continent, ten men have "been left by the Director" (p. 31). (Conrad delays telling us about them until midway through the story.) They belong "to a tribe from a very distant part of the land of darkness and sorrow," and do not try to escape, "naturally suppos[ing] that as wandering strangers they would be killed by the inhabitants of the country; in which they were right" (pp. 31–32). This "warlike tribe with filed teeth [...] had more grit" than to commit suicide and escape "the puzzling difficulties of existence". Thus they "went on stupidly living through disease and sorrow", do "very little work", and, like Kayerts and Carlier, grow sick and weak. From the interior they've come to the exterior and lost all their powers, pawns of colonialist practices, slaves to the Company and then slaves to the Loandans, who no doubt trade slaves to the colonialists and fellow Africans.

III. The Belgians

The three Belgians are the most clearly hierarchical – Managing Director, Station Chief, Station Chief's Assistant. For our two failures, colonialism offers a chance to redeem themselves. But instead disintegration sets in as soon as they've come into contact with the unknown. Rather than try to understand the natives, they prefer to mock and exploit them. "Carlier, smoking native tobacco in a short wooden pipe, would swagger up twirling his moustaches, and surveying the warriors with haughty indulgence, would say – 'Fine animals. Brought any bone? Yes?'" (p. 22) Significantly, it's not the natives that kill the two Belgians, but the Belgians themselves who are responsible for their own deaths, as isolated and foolish (that buffoonish collision, that protruding tongue) in death as they were in life.

What then of the Managing Director of the Great Civilizing Trading Company? His fondness for "grim humour" may link him to Conrad his creator, but the face of Kayerts "putting out a swollen tongue at his Managing Director" (p. 54) trumps him in the end, as it does us, and, perhaps, even Conrad.

Implications

If Conrad resembles the Managing Director of the Company with his own grim humour, then the irony of the final image lies, as I've just suggested, as hard on the author as it does on the Director. The heart of darkness for Conrad is both within and without, and it is inexplicable. Inexplicability – that is, our essential inability to comprehend – is what lies behind the encounter with the Other.

For Kayerts and Carlier, Africa is baffling, impenetrable, mysterious, and finally absurd. Beneath their colonial attitudes and actions, their assumed superiority over the primitive, Conrad presents a universe that at base is beyond anyone's capacity to understand. The source of Conrad's darkest irony is, then, epistemological. What is it we really know? Again and again Conrad emphasizes man's incomprehension. "Even the brilliant sunshine disclosed nothing intelligible" (p. 21). "Kayerts sat on his chair and looked down on the proceedings, understanding nothing" (p. 22). "The two men understood nothing, and cared for nothing but for the passage of days that separated them from the steamer's return" (p. 24). To them Gobila is "incomprehensible" (p. 26) and the speech of the Loandan traders "one of those impossible languages which sometimes we hear in our dreams" (p. 28).

The Africans understand as little as the Belgians. Gobila knows nothing about the white men and invests them with supernatural qualities, something we often do when confronted with the unknown. Though Makola can run the station better than Kayerts and Carlier, he can't understand the Loandans either, even though his wife is Loandan.

Nothing is clear; all remains enigmatic. "But about feelings people really know nothing. We talk with indignation or enthusiasm; we talk about oppression, cruelty, crime, devotion, self-sacrifice, virtue, and we know nothing real beyond the words" (pp. 38–39). Like the indentured slaves from the interior, we are baffled by "the puzzling difficulties of existence" and yet go on "stupidly living through disease and sorrow" (p. 32). The fog that lies over the station is a fitting image for their inability to see, to make distinctions; this *white* mist "clings and kills, the mist white and deadly, immaculate and poisonous", lies like a "white shroud [over] that land of sorrow" (p. 51).

That which we cannot understand we often fear, and in our fear either worship (Gobila the whites) or hate (Kayerts and Carlier the blacks). "A man may destroy everything within himself, love and hate and belief, and even doubt; but as long as he clings to life he cannot destroy fear: the fear, subtle, indestructible, and terrible, that pervades his being; that tinges his thoughts; that lurks in his heart; that watches on his lips the struggle of his last breath" (p. 40). Out of his ignorance and fear, "mild old Gobila offered extra human sacrifices to all the Evil Spirits that had taken possession of his white friends" (pp. 40–41). Out of his ignorance and fear, Carlier wants to "exterminat[e] all the niggers" (p. 42). In his fear Kayerts thinks that if he gives in to Carlier and lets him have a lump of sugar for his coffee, "he will begin this horror again tomorrow – and the day after – every day – raise other pretensions, trample on me, torture me, make me his slave – and I will be lost!" (p. 47). Then, out of his ignorance and fear, he shoots an unarmed man.

Early in the story Conrad comments:

> Few men realize that their life, the very essence of their character, their capabilities and their audacities, are only the expression of their belief in the safety of their surroundings. The courage, the composure, the confidence; the emotions and principles, every great and every insignificant thought belongs not to the individual but to the crowd: to the crowd that believes blindly in the irresistible force of its institutions and of its morals, in the power of its police and of its opinion. But the contact with pure unmitigated savagery, with primitive nature and primitive man, brings sudden and profound trouble into the heart […] a suggestion of things vague, uncontrollable, and repulsive, whose discomposing intrusion excites the imagination and tries the civilized nerves of the foolish and the wise alike. (p. 17)

This passage states the story's general conflict (the encounter of the civilized with the primitive) and points us to its development ("tries the nerves of the foolish"). It also contains what appears to be a cynic's attitude toward society. But Conrad's attitude, no matter how dark, is never nihilistic. Instead the reader experiences the author's struggle to give a true account of what it means to be human. The artist, he tells us in the "Preface" to The Nigger of the "Narcissus ",

> speaks to our capacity for delight and wonder, to the sense of mystery surrounding our lives; to our sense of pity, and beauty, and pain; to the latent feeling of fellowship with all creation – to the subtle but invincible conviction of solidarity that knits together the loneliness of innumerable hearts, to the solidarity in dreams, in joy, in sorrow, in aspirations, in illusions, in hope, in fear, which binds men to each other, which binds together all humanity – the dead to the living and the living to the unborn.

Yes, contradictions, paradoxes, unknowability, inconclusions dominate the story, and everything remains unsettled up to and even beyond death. The tongue sticking out at the Director in the end appears to mock everything the Director stands for, but the worse insult may be that its true meaning is beyond our means to comprehend.

Background Information: Colonialism, Racism, and Conrad

If what Conrad paints on his dark canvas seems lurid (the purple cheek, the protruding tongue), it's there to sink us deeper into the vortex of its contrarieties, not to cater to one or the other side in the battle between the I and the Other. Conrad had colonialism's number down long before anyone could have ever dreamed of post-colonialism, in relation to which current of thought he stands at the forefront or outpost. In "An Outpost of Progress" colonialism is represented by the Great Trading (Civilizing) Company; in Victory (1915) it's the equally pointed Tropical Belt Coal Company; and in Heart of Darkness (first published in Blackwood's Magazine in 1899) we have the International Society for the Suppression of Savage Customs. Underneath Conrad's irony a strong sense of morality obtains. In the "Author's Note" to Victory he tells us that he is a writer "without any moral intention [except] that which pervades the whole scheme of this world of senses." "The conquest of the earth," says Marlow in Heart of Darkness, "which mostly means the taking it away from those who have a different complexion or slightly flatter noses than ourselves, is not a pretty thing when you look into it too much." But Conrad's project is to make us "look … too much."

It may, then, come as a surprise to some readers to hear in Chinua Achebe's 1977 essay "An Image of Africa" Conrad called "a thoroughgoing racist". That Conrad did not explore the interior life of Africans or women is, for the most part, true. Whether this was due to racism and sexism, however, is somewhat more problematic. Achebe, for example, notes that in *Heart of Darkness* Marlow narrates his story while on the River Thames, but that where the story takes place, "the River Congo, [is] the very antithesis of the Thames." Does such differentiation exist at the heart of Conrad's darkness? At the end of that short novel, Achebe seems to have forgotten, it is the Thames, not the Congo, that "seemed to lead into the heart of an immense darkness."

For the novelist Wilson Harris of Guyana, Conrad understood the "necessity for distortions" to critique colonialism's hegemony. Likewise the Ugandan author Peter Nazareth praises Conrad as "a mental liberator: not only for those blinded at home but also for those who were to come later, the colonized elite wearing the eyes of Europe" (Wilson and Nazareth as quoted in Robert Hamner's essay "The Enigma of Arrival in 'An Outpost of Progress'" (*Conradiana*, Fall 2001, Vol. 33 No. 1)). "In 'An Outpost of Progress,'" notes Ian Watt, "Conrad was primarily concerned with the colonizers, and there the general purport of his fiction is consistent and unequivocal: imperial or colonial experience is disastrous for the whites; it makes them lazy; it reveals their weaknesses; it puffs them up with empty vanity at being white; and it fortifies the intolerable hypocrisy with which Europeans in general conceal their selfish aims" (*Conrad in the Nineteenth Century*, 1979).

Rather than accuse Conrad of racism or sexism, we might, as John Lyon says in his introduction to *Youth/Heart of Darkness/The End of the Tether*, "find something principled, rather than evasive, in the Conrad who at his best refuses to claim to comprehend, and in an art which enacts the costly drama of such incomprehension." Regarding those critics like Edward Said who say that Conrad, as much as he critiqued imperialism, performed the imperialistic trick of projecting false images of the Other onto the screen of westernized eyes, we should recall that for Conrad – born of Polish parents in Russian-controlled Ukraine and whose family, for political reasons, was exiled to Volagda in northern Russia where his mother died when he was seven – there was no dearth of countries in which to portray mankind's inhumanity.

The harshness of Conrad's critique of colonialism hardly masks the author's moral outrage. But was it as thorough as it should have been? Not for Achebe and others. Perhaps, however, to critique Conrad's writing at the end of the 19th century by the standards of critics of the late 20th century is a bit facile. "If Conrad," as Robert Hamner says, "often appears inattentive to the consciousness of non-Europeans, he relentlessly carves away the illusions behind Western exploitation of the 'other.'" What John Lyon says of *Heart of Darkness* is equally applicable to "An Outpost of Progress": "the values of European cultures are revealed as sustained only at the cost of the subjugation of other races, and those very values are often violated in the course of that subjugation" and are "often merely sham, values to which lip-service is paid in the interest of uglier ends."

The veneer of civilization hangs over "An Outpost of Progress" like the thick fog does at the story's end, and when the fog lifts we see the emptiness beneath the veneer. Whether the Conrad character responds to this emptiness by embracing nihilism, suicide, cynicism, colonialism, or racism, Conrad's art succumbs to none of them, as his epigraph to *Youth: A Narrative; and Two Other Stories* (1902) attests: "... But the Dwarf answered: No; something human is dearer to me than the wealth of all the world." – *Grimm's Tales*

For an overview of the charge of racism brought by Achebe against Conrad, see John Lyon's "Introduction" to the Penguin edition of *Youth/Heart of Darkness/The End of the Tether* (1995).

Teaching Suggestions

Pre-Reading Activities

1. Locate on a map the three African countries mentioned in the story: the Congo, where the story takes place; Loanda (Luanda, on the South Atlantic coast of Nigeria), where the armed traders in the story come from; Sierra Leone (on the North Atlantic coast), home country of Makola who runs, in all but name, the Company station. And, as long as we're looking at a map, ask the students what they know about recent events in troubled regions of Africa such as the Darfur region of Sudan, Ethiopia, Eritrea, Somali, Rwanda, Liberia, Zimbabwe, etc.

2. Since the principal moral issue in the story is slavery, ask the students to discuss exactly what they find wrong about it.

While-Reading Activity

Have part of the class note the passages of ironic commentary, another group instances of Conrad's concrete descriptions, another the main points of the narrative structure: exposition, conflicts within the rising action, the climax (two-thirds through the story), the falling action, and denouement. (See discussion above in the sections on "Narrative Structure" and "Language".)

After-Reading Activities /Analysis

1. In order to better understand the effects of the cross-cultural dynamics at work in "An Outpost of Progress," have the students list the character traits of the three Belgian characters, the three African characters, and the two African groups in the story. (See above section on "Characterization and the Effects of Colonialism".)

2. The director of the Great Trading Company is said to indulge in a "grim humour". So does the story's auctorial voice. Cite instances of this. (Conrad's "grim humour" is clearest in the story's grotesque final image. For instances of "grim humour" in the auctorial narration see above section on "Language: Description and Irony".)

Topics for Class Discussion

1. As Conrad wrote in his preface to The Nigger of the "Narcissus", "All art [...] appeals primarily to the senses, and the artistic aim when expressing itself in written words must also make its appeal through the senses, if its high desire is to reach the secret spring of responsive emotions. [...] My task which I am trying to achieve is, by the power of the written word, to make you hear, to make you feel – it is, before all, to make you see. That – and no more, and it is everything." Discuss in what ways Conrad achieved this aim in "An Outpost of Progress".

2. Discuss the relationship of the story's narrative structure and the disintegration of Kayerts and Carlier. (See above section on "Narrative Structure" and "Characterization".)

Creative Writing

Many of Conrad's scenes are vividly rendered, as if ready-made for film. Have the students choose a scene of their choice and rewrite it as part of a screenplay.

Composition

1. At the beginning of the story we see the Director of the Company leaving the station, at the end his arrival. What is the purpose and effect of this framing device?

2. Discuss the function of irony in "An Outpost of Progress".

3. Writing about Heart of Darkness, John Lyon said that "the values of European cultures are revealed as [...] often merely sham, values to which lip-service is paid in the interest of uglier ends." The same can be said of the earlier story "An Outpost of Progress". Discuss the "uglier ends" of colonialism as they are presented in the story.

Topics for Presentations

1. Give a short report on the history of Belgium's occupation of the Congo.

Adam Hochschild, *King Leopold's Ghost* (Mariner Books,1999).

Neal Ascherson, *The King Incorporated: Leopold II in the Age of Trusts* (Doubleday, 1964).

"In the Heart of Darkness", by Adam Hochschild. *New York Review of Books*, Volume 52, Number 15 (October 6, 2005) Review of *Memory of Congo: The Colonial Era*, an exhibition at the Royal Museum for Central Africa, Tervuren, Belgium, February 4–October 9, 2005 and *La mémoire du Congo: Le temps colonial*, catalog of the exhibition, in French or Dutch, edited by Jean-Luc Vellut et al. Ghent and Tervuren: Éditions Snoeck/Musée royal de l'Afrique centrale.

http://www.nybooks.com/articles/article-preview?article_id=18305

http://en.wikipedia.org/wiki/Belgian_Congo

2. Give a presentation on the practice of slavery in Africa by Africans.

Paul E. Lovejoy, *Transformations in Slavery: A History of Slavery in Africa* (Cambridge University Press, 2000)

Synopsis: This history of slavery in Africa from the fifteenth to the early twentieth century examines how indigenous African slavery developed within an international context. Professor Lovejoy discusses the medieval Islamic slave trade and the Atlantic trade as well as the process of enslavement and the marketing of slaves. He considers the impact of European abolition and assesses slavery's role in African history. The book corrects the accepted interpretation that African slavery was mild and resulted in the slaves' assimilation. Instead, slaves were used extensively in production, although the exploitation methods and the relationships to world markets differed from those in the Americas. Nevertheless, slavery in Africa, like slavery in the Americas, developed from its position on the periphery of capitalist Europe. The new edition revises all statistical material on the slave trade demography and incorporates recent research with an updated bibliography. (from Amazon.co.uk)

3. Discuss Chinua Achebe's labeling Conrad a "racist".

See pp. 324 - 327 of *The Many Voices of English* and pp. xxxv - xlii ("Conrad, theory and politics") by John Lyon from his "Introduction" to *Youth/Heart of Darkness/The End of the Tether* (London: Penguin, 1995).

Somerset Maugham
"The Force of Circumstance" (1924)

Interpretation and Background Information

Short Summary and Interpretation of "The Force of Circumstance"

At the outset Maugham presents his exotic setting from the point of view (third person limited) of a young British woman, Doris, wife of Guy, chief of a trading station in Southeast Asia, thus drawing his readers into the colonial world and at the same time establishing a contrast between it and the home country. The "mellifluous and rich" song of a native bird, causes Doris to think "for an instant, with a catch at her heart [. . .] of the English blackbird" (pp. 56–57). Many elements in the opening paragraph such as the colours – "ashy" and "wan" compared to "a melody in minor key which exacerbates the nerves by its ambiguous monotony"; p. 56) belie the wife's apparent happiness. Elements of foreboding run throughout the story and, coupled with Doris's ignorance, recall the dramatic irony found in Greek tragedies.

Guy, who has grown up in Sembulu, met Doris when she was on holiday at the British seaside. It is his personality ("a gay, jolly little man"; p. 58) rather than his looks ("a red face like the full moon", "rather pimply" p. 57) that attracts her. "When she was with him she felt happy and good-tempered" (p. 58).

Their relationship appears characterized more by comradeship than romantic love. Both of them are "shy of displaying emotion" and rarely use "with one another anything but ironic banter" (p. 66). The description of their married life reflects the colonialists' desire to export British culture to the colonies. Thus Doris uses her wedding presents to make the house "habitable" (p. 65), i.e. more English, and Guy pours Worcester sauce over his food to make it "palatable" (p. 62). Both of them eagerly await the English newspapers, magazines and books brought to them once a month by steamer, and they have established the very British routine of playing tennis and drinking gin slings in the early afternoon.

Into this scene of apparent colonial and marital bliss, Maugham introduces a native woman who keeps *waylaying* Guy in the bathhouse (p. 59).

> She was slight and small, with the large, dark, starry eyes of her race and a mass of raven hair. She did not stir as they went by, but stared at them strangely. Doris saw then that she was not quite so young as she had at first thought. Her features were a trifle heavy and her skin was dark, but she was very pretty. She held a small child in her arms. Doris smiled a little as she saw it, but no answering smile moved the woman's lips. (p. 67)

The reader, though not Doris, is quick to suspect that a sexual relationship between Guy and this woman once existed. Ironically, Doris comes close to the truth when she says: "I'm thankful you never had a Malay wife. I should have hated it. Just think if those two little brats were yours" (p. 62). Only after half the story is over does Guy reveal to Doris that prior to his marriage he has lived with and had three children by this native woman (pp. 73–79).

Doris does not burst out in a fit of jealousy, as one might expect, but remains calm, self-contained, and does her best to conceal her emotions. She simply demands the right to withdraw to her room. Upon further reflection and after a period of six months, however, she decides to leave her husband and travel back to England. It is a very subtle form of racism rather than jealousy that drives her away – her revulsion at imagining her husband having had a sexual relationship with a coloured wife. As she herself explains: "It's a physical thing, I can't help it, it's stronger than I am. I think of those thin black arms of hers round you and it fills me with a physical nausea." (pp. 86–87). Resigned to his fate, Guy lets his wife go and in the end welcomes the native woman and his children back into his home.

Racism and Miscegenation

For today's readers it might be difficult to understand why race plays such an important role in the story's relationships, why Guy deliberately travels to Britain to find an English wife, and why he so readily discards the native woman as soon as a white woman is available. After all, he has three children with his 'Malay wife' and there is no indication that their relationship deteriorates or that they quarrel. The only explanation one can find is either that Guy does not love and has never loved the native woman in the same way he loves Doris, that he has put up with her presence in order not to be alone, has used her to comfort him (almost like a pet) or that he has internalized racism and the prevalent ideology of the British Empire not to interfere with native women to such an extent that this prevents him from seeing her as a full human being to be treated with respect, a prerequisite for true love. With Doris he has an entirely different relationship. He respects her feelings, or at least seems to understand her disgust at the thought of miscegenation, and concurs with her ultimate decision to go back to England. In accordance with the ideology of the Empire his Malay wife accepts her inferior position and readily comes back after Doris has left. *Hot tears trickle down Guy's funny, round spotty face* (cf. p. 92) as he surrenders to the force of circumstance and informs her son that he would like his 'native wife' to come back.

Point of View

Although the story is told by an omniscient narrator, it is not a neutral, impartial observer, but an empathic one who takes over the protagonists' perspectives from time to time. Thus the depiction of the tropical setting is influenced by Doris's point of view (cf. pp. 56–57 and pp. 63–64) and Guy's disclosure (pp. 73–79) is delivered in first-person. In general, the point of view is third person limited omniscience, with the first half limited to Doris's perspective and the last half seen from Guy's. This allows Maugham to give the reader a balanced view of the events, permitting him to avoid passing judgement on the morality (or lack thereof) of Guy's actions or Doris's reaction (or over-reaction) to it.

Foreshadowing and (Tragic) Irony

"The Force of Circumstance" contains several instances of foreshadowing which are also examples of tragic irony. In a general sense, irony denotes an incongruity between what a writer or speaker says and what is understood. In ancient Greek drama, tragic or dramatic irony occurs when a character onstage is ignorant, but the audience knows his or her eventual fate. Several times in Maugham's story Doris speaks of the mixed-blood children in the village and their mother but does not realize they are her husband's offspring. The reader knows more than Doris.

After the native woman appears at the house for the first time, Doris comments on Guy's talk with the woman, who, in her eyes is a stranger:

> "It's lucky I'm not a suspicious or a jealous person. (...) I don't know that I should altogether approve of your having animated conversations with ladies while you're having your bath." (p. 60)

Although Doris is serious, albeit light-hearted here, her statement must seem ironic to Guy as well as to the reader.

Blissfully ignorant of her husband's three children, Doris tells her husband that she has met two half-castes in the village, who, as it later turns out, are Guy's sons. Her husband, however, skillfully avoids the issue without directly lying:

> "Oh, Guy, there were two little boys watching him who were much whiter than the others. I wondered if they were half-castes. I spoke to them, but they didn't know a word of English."
> "There are two or three half-caste children in the kampong," he answered.
> "Who do they belong to?"
> "Their mother is one of the village girls."
> "Who is their father?"
> "Oh, my dear, that's the sort of question we think is a little dangerous to ask out here. He paused ."A lot of fellows have native wives, and then when they go home or marry they pension them off and send them back to their village." (p. 61)

As they continue to discuss the issue, Doris finally makes the following comment:

> "I'm not hard. But I'm thankful you never had a Malay wife. I should have hated it. Just think if those two little brats were yours." (p. 62)

This constitutes the height of tragic irony in the story.

A little later, she reiterates her fears:

> "I'm very lucky to have caught you so young. Honestly, it would upset me dreadfully if I were told that you had lived like that." (p. 63)

Probably in order to change the subject, Guy asks her: "Are you happy here, darling?" and she answers: "Desperately." (p. 63) The adjective 'desperately' has a positive sense here, meaning 'very much', but underneath the surface the negative energy of the word's original meaning 'desperate' (i.e. 'hopeless') remains, ironically foreshadowing the despair Doris will suffer after she has learned about her husband's previous relationship with the Malay woman.

Even though, as the story progresses, the hints become more and more disturbing, Doris turns a deaf ear to them. When she sees the native woman again, she thinks: "What a pretty sarong she's got. (...) I wonder where it comes from." (p. 67), probably understanding that it must have been a present from a wealthy white person, but not yet making the connection between the woman's frequent appearances at her house, her children of mixed race and Guy.

A little later, when Doris and Guy speak about the woman again, Guy gives himself away by indicating the exact age of the child, but Doris still does not understand, although she wonders how he could possibly know…

> "It was horrible to see a woman treated like that. She had a baby in her arms."
> "Hardly a baby. It's three years old."
> "How d'you know?"
> "I know all about her." (p. 72)

Symbolism: Landscape Descriptions, the Chik-chak and the River

Landscape Descriptions

The story's opening scene gives a vivid impression of the setting. However, a sensitive reader will not overlook the dissonant tones alluding to death and destruction:

> She was sitting on the veranda waiting for her husband to come in for luncheon. The Malay boy had drawn the blinds when the morning lost its freshness, but she had partly raised one of them so that she could look at the river. Under the breathless sun of midday it had the white pallor of death. A native was paddling along in a dug-out so small that it hardly showed above the surface of the water. The colours of the day were ashy and wan. They were but the various tones of the heat. (It was like an Eastern melody, in the minor key, which exacerbates the nerves by its ambiguous monotony; and the ear awaits impatiently a resolution, but waits in vain.) The cicadas sang their grating song with a frenzied energy; it was as continual and monotonous as the rustling of a brook over the stones; but on a sudden it was drowned by the loud singing of a bird, mellifluous and rich; and for an instant, with a catch at her heart, she thought of the English blackbird. (pp. 56–57)

The description of this tropical landscape is influenced by Doris's point of view (she has raised one of the blinds, so that she can look out at the river) and is charged with premonition. It is not a romantic setting idealizing the tropical and the foreign, but contains many negative elements. The midday sun is "breathless" (you may want to point out to your students the use here of a transferred epithet; the air, not the sun, is "breathless", i.e. it's so hot one can't breathe). The river has "the white pallor of death" and the day's colours – "ashy" and "wan" – are deathly as well.

The acoustic accompaniment of the setting is also negative. The day's colours are compared to a melody in a sombre minor key that *exacerbates* one's nerves; one *waits impatiently for a resolution,* which never occurs. The cicadas' song is "grating" and "frenzied".

The only positive element of this description is the mellifluous song of a bird, distantly reminding Doris of the English blackbird. It seems like a glimmer of hope in a hostile environment – just like the marriage at first appears like an exotic escape from Doris's dreary existence as a secretary and the large responsibility that rests on her shoulders as the only custodian of her mother.

In a flashback the second depiction of a tropical landscape informs us about the couple's arrival in Malay:

> When a little coasting steamer set them down at the mouth of the river, where a large boat, manned by a dozen Dyaks, was waiting to take them to the station, her breath was taken away by the beauty, friendly rather than awe-inspiring, of the scene. It had a gaiety, like the joyful singing of birds in the trees, which she had never expected. On each bank of the river were mangroves and nipah palms, and behind them the dense green of the forest. In the distance stretched blue mountains, range upon range, as far as the eye could see. She had no sense of confinement nor of gloom, but rather of openness and wide spaces where the exultant fancy could wander with delight. The green glittered in the sunshine and the sky was blithe and cheerful. The gracious land seemed to offer her a gracious welcome.
> They rowed on, hugging a bank, and high overhead flew a pair of doves. A flash of colour, like a living jewel, dashed across their path. It was a kingfisher. Two monkeys, with their dangling tails, sat side by side on a branch. On the horizon, over there on the other side of the broad and turbid river, beyond the jungle, was a row of little white clouds in the sky, and they looked like a row of ballet-girls, dressed in white, waiting at the back of the stage, alert and merry, for the curtain to go up. (pp. 63–64)

To Doris (and the narrative perspective is clearly influenced by Doris's point of view here) the landscape seems paraddisaical. Positive adjectives and nouns, such as "beauty", "friendly", "gaiety", "joyful", "blithe", "cheerful", "gracious" (used twice in one sentence) underline the scene's beauty. This is a typical foreigner's perspective, one that fails to see things as they really are, by either romanticizing or demonizing them. In Doris's case glorification has clearly taken the upper hand. Her perception of the landscape contrasts vividly with the matter-of-fact, geographical, but also slightly threatening depiction of the Malay Archipelago she has read about in novels prior to her arrival, in which the land is described as "sombre", "with great ominous rivers and a silent, impenetrable jungle" (p. 63).

The animals, too, are portrayed as beautiful and peaceful. The kingfisher's flight is compared to "a dash of colour" and two monkeys sit peacefully side by side on a tree dangling their tails.

The fanciful, self-reflexive simile of the clouds "like a row of ballet-girls" waiting backstage underscores Doris's naiveté. When the curtain rises for her, when the veil of illusion is lifted, it won't be a children's ballet she sees.

The Chik-chak

The croak of the chik-chak is mentioned for the first time within Guy's first-person-narrative as he recalls the intense pangs of loneliness he used to feel in the evening after the native boys had returned to the kampong. There is a strong contrast between the natives' sociability and his feelings of isolation as the only white person.

> After dinner the boys shut up and went away to sleep in the kampong. I was all alone. There wasn't a sound in the bungalow except now and then the croak of the chik-chak. It used to come out of the silence, suddenly, so that it made me jump. Over in the kampong

I heard the sound of a gong or fire-crackers. They were having a good time, they weren't so far away, but I had to stay where I was. (p. 75)

When Doris announces her final decision to leave Guy and go back to England, the chik-chak reappears:

> For two minutes perhaps she [Doris] sat there without a word. She started when the chik-chak gave its piercing, hoarse, and strangely human cry. Guy rose and went out on to the veranda. He leaned against the rail and looked at the softly flowing water. (p. 88)

Here too the chik-chak is associated with Guy's state of mind. Upon hearing Doris's final decision he is shocked and its piercing and strangely human cry mirrors his despair at her departure. Once she has left, he will be faced with his loneliness and isolation again. Note, however, that this time Doris's reaction to the chik-chak is described, too – she is startled by it. It is as if through its croak Doris is reminded of Guy's former life with the native woman, as if already at that point of the story the native woman calls him back after it has become clear that Doris will leave.

In the end the chik-chak mocks Guy's decision to set up house with the native woman again.

> The chik-chak was noisy that night and its hoarse and sudden cry seemed to mock him. You could hardly believe that this reverberating sound came from so small a throat. Presently he heard a discreet cough.
> "Who's there?" he cried.
> There was a pause. He looked at the door. The chik-chak laughed harshly. A small boy sidled in and stood on the threshold. It was a little half-caste boy in a tattered singlet and a sarong. It was the elder of his two sons. (p. 91)

The chik-chak serves as a leitmotif mirroring Guy's feelings of despair and loneliness. In the end it assumes a life of its own and makes fun of the protagonist who bows to the force of circumstance.

The River

As we've seen, Maugham in the first paragraph associates the river with death ("it had the white pallor of death"; p. 56). When Doris and Guy come back home from the tennis court and Guy mixes a couple of gin slings for them, the river is mentioned again, but this time parts of it are mysteriously concealed by the approaching night, just as the future is unknown to Doris and Guy at this point in the story:

> The river stretched widely before them, and on the further bank the jungle was wrapped in the mystery of the approaching night. A native was silently rowing up-stream, standing at the bow of the boat, with two oars. (p. 69)

A little later the river's presence increases in intensity:

> At their feet, with a mighty, formidable sluggishness, silent, mysterious and fatal, flowed the river. It had the terrible deliberation and the relentlessness of destiny. (p. 73)

After this premonitory description of the river Guy discloses his secret to his wife and informs her about his previous relationship with the Malay woman and their three children. Furthermore, Maugham draws a parallel between the river and destiny, a connection that is fitting for any passage in which the river is mentioned and is especially appropriate just before Guy utters the fateful sentence: "Doris, I've got something to say to you." (p. 73).

After Doris has announced her final decision to leave and Guy has given his consent to her departure, *he leans against the rail and looks at the softly flowing water (p. 88)*, knowing that he cannot change his fate, but is merely a bystander watching destiny unfold. The next morning, after Doris has packed up all her belongings, Guy asks: "Would you like me to come to the mouth of the river with you?" and Doris answers: "Oh, I think it would be better if we said good-bye here." (p. 89), as if wanting to spare him the trouble of being confronted with his fate, symbolized by the river. When Doris actually leaves, the river is described as "ghostly" (p. 89) and a little afterwards we read: "The dawn now was creeping along the river mistily" (p. 90). Once again, both Doris's and Guy's fates are veiled in the mist of their unknown futures.

Teaching Suggestions

Pre-Reading Activity

"Igorance is bliss."

– Discuss this saying. What are the advantages and disadvantages of not knowing about something?

– Do you think there are cases where it is better not to know?

– Should you always tell the truth or can you think of examples where it is fair not to tell the truth to protect somebody from harm?

While-Reading Activities

1. How might the story continue? (class participation)

Have the students read the story up to p. 61, l. 8: "He smiled, but Doris, with the quick perception of a woman in love, noticed that he smiled only with his lips, not as usual with his eyes also, and wondered what it was that troubled him."
– Doris realizes that something is wrong, but does not know what it is. What do you think might be reasons for Guy's strange reaction to the native woman?
Collect possible reasons on the board and discuss their likeliness with the class. With a raised awareness of the story's possible outcomes, the students then go on reading.

2. Monologue of Guy (writing activity)

Go on reading the story up to p. 73, l. 24: "Doris, I've got something to say to you." For homework/ in groups make the students write a monologue of Guy, in which he discloses something to his wife. Then have one member of the group come to the front and read and act out his disclosure to the class. After a couple of students have presented their speeches, have them read the rest of the story and contrast their anticipated speeches with Maugham's story.

After-Reading Activities / Analysis

1. Tragic irony

Explain the terms 'foreshadowing' and 'tragic irony' to the students. After they have read the whole story, make the students reread the story and look for instances of tragic irony which foreshadow Guy's confession about his relationship with the Malay woman.

2. Group Work on the Story's Symbolism

In groups have the students analyze the setting, the chik-chak and the river with the aid of copymasters 1, 2 and 3.

3. Characterization

Split the class into four groups. Group one takes notes for a characterization of Doris, group two for a characterization of Guy, group three takes a closer look at their relationship and group four takes a look at how the native woman is presented in the text. Tell the class to distinguish between direct and indirect characterization. Hand out posters and felt-tips. Allow about twenty to thirty minutes for this, then have the students present their results.

4. Going native / Clash of cultures

a) Find instances in the story where Guy and Doris go native and, the other way around, export British culture to the colonies.

Doris and Guy do their very best to bring British culture to Malay – playing tennis, reading English newspapers, redecorating the house in English style, drinking gin slings in the late afternoon, pouring Worcester sauce over native dishes. However, we learn that Doris is "industriously learning the language" (p. 70) – her form of going native, whereas Guy has chosen the most extreme form of going native, having a relationship with a native woman, before Doris's arrival and will do so again after she has left. After Doris's departure we see him wearing native dress again even before the native woman comes back to his house. Having been born in Sembulu, he seems to feel more at home in Malay than in England.

b) Discussion: What do you think? Should you stick to your own culture or should you adapt to the customs of your new country when living abroad?

5. Explain the story's title "The Force of Circumstance" with reference to the three protagonists, Guy, Doris and the native woman.

In Maugham's words, Guy surrenders (p. 92) to the force of circumstance at the end of the story again. Having suffered from acute loneliness he had arranged for a Malay woman to live with him and ends up spending ten years of his life with her. He then goes to England to find a white wife and after only four weeks of vacation is lucky enough to find Doris. He pretends to love her deeply. However, it seems odd that he finds a wife so quickly after he has made up his mind to marry. In a sense, Doris thus becomes the victim of circumstance, too – of his wish to marry a white woman. Guy's decision to look for an English wife, however, makes him the victim of imperial ideology, which has instilled in him that only a union with a white woman is a good one and represents a proper marriage since coloured women are regarded as inferior.

The Malay woman is a victim of circumstance, too. She is offered to the white man because her family is poor and needs the money and later on is dependent on Guy for the well-being of her children. She is the victim of the circumstances of colonial rule.

Doris, too, suffers from the force of circumstance. After she has learned about Guy's past, her English upbringing and values make it impossible for her to stay with her husband although they love each other. According to her ideology it is impossible to marry a white woman after having gone native. She is repelled at the thought of Guy having embraced a coloured woman. ("I think of those thin black arms of hers round you and it fills me with physical nausea." (pp. 86–87). The question whether she would have reacted the same way had Guy had a previous relationship with a white woman – whether jealousy or racism is the underlying motive for her actions – remains unanswered.

Topics for Class Discussion

1. (True) Love?

Read out the following quotation from the story to the students:

> "I sent her back to the village before I left here. I told her it was all over. I gave her what I'd promised. She always knew it was only a temporary arrangement. I was fed up with it. I told her I was going to marry a white woman."
>
> "But you hadn't even seen me then."
>
> "No, I know. But I'd made up my mind to marry when I was home." (pp. 77–78)

Then ask the following questions to open up class discussion:

– Who does Guy really love? Doris or the native woman?

– Is he capable of love at all?

– Does he really love his children?

– What do you think are Guy's reasons for marrying an English woman after he has gone native for so long and has already had three children with a Malay woman?

– Can you understand that Doris leaves her husband or not? Is she right or is she really a 'hysterical brat' as she refers to herself in the text?

– Does the fact that his relationship with the native woman would not be appreciated by the Empire prevent him from having true emotions for her? Or does he really not have any true feelings for her and simply uses her sexually to allay his loneliness?

Creative Writing

Filling in the gaps: Dialogue in the bathhouse

Although we know that the native woman must be angry at Guy and tries to get him back, we are never told what she is saying in her native tongue. Merely through the tone of her voice can we guess what she must be talking about.

Let's assume she is speaking in English for a moment. Make up the dialogue between her and Guy in the bath-house where, in Guy's words, she is *waylaying* him.

Composition

Comparisons with Other Stories

1. In a way Guy gives up his own children when saying that he doesn't have any deep feelings for them ("the honest truth is that they're no more to me than if they were somebody else's children."; p. 79). Compare his behaviour to Lou Parker's decision to give her baby up for adoption in Spark's "The Black Madonna". What differences and similarities do you see?

2. In Maugham's "The Force of Circumstance" Guy and Doris have a very indirect way of interacting with each other and conceal rather than show their feelings. Compare the interaction between these two spouses with the way Ayub and Begum treat each other in Shahraz's story "A Pair of Jeans".

Topics for Presentations

1. **The Malay Archipelago**
   Prepare a presentation on the Malay Archipelago. (This topic is especially suitable for students with an interest in geography, biology or politics.)
   The following web sites might prove helpful:
   http://en.wikipedia.org/wiki/Malay_Archipelago
   http://encarta.msn.com/map_701514414/Malay_Archipelago.html
   http://www.wku.edu/~smithch/wallace/S078.htm

2. **Going Native**
   Prepare a presentation on the concept of going native. You may want to go to the following web site:
   http://www.qub.ac.uk/en/imperial/key-concepts/Going-native.htm

3. **Different Forms of Irony**
   Have one student/a group of students prepare a talk on different forms of irony. The following web site gives an excellent overview of the history and various uses and forms of irony. Moreover, it offers a multitude of examples.
   http://en.wikipedia.org/wiki/Irony

4. **Additional Reading**
   Have the students/one student read Rudyard Kipling's story "Georgie Porgie". Make them compare it to Somerset Maugham's "The Force of Circumstance", especially with respect to the concept of going native. Also try to find out the two authors' attitudes towards this practice and compare the ways in which the two native women and their relationships with a white man are portrayed.
   (This might also be a suitable topic for the presentation of one student. In Baden-Württemberg this topic also lends itself as a GFS *(gleichwertige Feststellung von Schülerleistungen)*.

Copymaster 1

GROUP WORK:
Symbolism in "The Force of Circumstance"

GROUP I: Setting

Take a look at the snippets below. They all have to do with the story's setting. Analyse them and relate them to the characters' states of mind at different points of the story.

Answer the following questions.

– **Which descriptions are influenced by one person's point of view, which are seen from an omniscient perspective?**

– **In which way does the setting mirror the feelings of one or more characters at a particular point of the story? (You may want to look at the context of the quotation for this.)**

– **List positive and negative elements of the description and try to interpret them.**

She was sitting on the veranda waiting for her husband to come in for luncheon. The Malay boy had drawn the blinds when the morning lost its freshness, but she had partly raised one of them so that she could look at the river. Under the breathless sun of midday it had the white pallor of death. A native was paddling along in a dug-out so small that it hardly showed above the surface of the water. The colours of the day were ashy and wan. They were but the various tones of the heat. (It was like an Eastern melody, in the minor key, which exacerbates the nerves by its ambiguous monotony; and the ear awaits impatiently a resolution, but waits in vain.) The cicadas sang their grating song with a frenzied energy; it was as continual and monotonous as the rustling of a brook over the stones; but on a sudden it was drowned by the loud singing of a bird, mellifluous and rich; and for an instant, with a catch at her heart, she thought of the English blackbird. (pp. 56–57)

When a little coasting steamer set them down at the mouth of the river, where a large boat, manned by a dozen Dyaks, was waiting to take them to the station, her breath was taken away by the beauty, friendly rather than awe-inspiring, of the scene. It had a gaiety, like the joyful singing of birds in the trees, which she had never expected. On each bank of the river were mangroves and nipah palms, and behind them the dense green of the forest. In the distance stretched blue mountains, range upon range, as far as the eye could see. She had no sense of confinement nor of gloom, but rather of openness and wide spaces where the exultant fancy could wander with delight. The green glittered in the sunshine and the sky was blithe and cheerful. The gracious land seemed to offer her a gracious welcome.
They rowed on, hugging a bank, and high overhead flew a pair of doves. A flash of colour, like a living jewel, dashed across their path. It was a kingfisher. Two monkeys, with their dangling tails, sat side by side on a branch. On the horizon, over there on the other side of the broad and turbid river, beyond the jungle, was a row of little white clouds in the sky, and they looked like a row of ballet-girls, dressed in white, waiting at the back of the stage, alert and merry, for the curtain to go up. (pp. 63–64)

GROUP WORK:
Symbolism in "The Force of Circumstance"

GROUP II: The chik-chak

Take a look at the snippets below. They all have to do with the story's setting. Analyse them and relate them to the characters' states of mind at different points of the story.

Answer the following questions.

– Which descriptions are influenced by one person's point of view, which are seen from an omniscient perspective?

– In which way does the setting mirror the feelings of one or more characters at a particular point of the story? (You may want to look at the context of the quotation for this.)

– List positive and negative elements of the description and try to interpret them.

After dinner the boys shut up and went away to sleep in the kampong. I was all alone. There wasn't a sound in the bungalow except now and then the croak of the chik-chak. It used to come out of the silence, suddenly, so that it made me jump. Over in the kampong I heard the sound of a gong or fire-crackers. They were having a good time, they weren't so far away, but I had to stay where I was. (p. 75)

For two minutes perhaps she [Doris] sat there without a word. She started when the chik-chak gave its piercing, hoarse, and strangely human cry. Guy rose and went out on to the veranda. He leaned against the rail and looked at the softly flowing water. (p. 88)

The chik-chak was noisy that night and its hoarse and sudden cry seemed to mock him. You could hardly believe that this reverberating sound came from so small a throat. Presently he heard a discreet cough.
"Who's there?" he cried.
There was a pause. He looked at the door. The chik-chak laughed harshly. A small boy sidled in and stood on the threshold. It was a little half-caste boy in a tattered singlet and a sarong. It was the elder of his two sons. (p. 91)

GROUP WORK:
Symbolism in "The Force of Circumstance"

GROUP II: The river

Take a look at the snippets below. They all have to do with the story's setting. Analyse them and relate them to the characters' states of mind at different points of the story.

Answer the following questions.

– **Which descriptions are influenced by one person's point of view, which are seen from an omniscient perspective?**

– **In which way does the setting mirror the feelings of one or more characters at a particular point of the story? (You may want to look at the context of the quotation for this.)**

– **List positive and negative elements of the description and try to interpret them.**

Under the breathless sun of midday it [the river] had the white pallor of death. (p. 56)

The river stretched widely before them, and on the further bank the jungle was wrapped in the mystery of the approaching night. A native was silently rowing up-stream, standing at the bow of the boat, with two oars. (p. 69)

At their feet, with a mighty, formidable sluggishness, silent, mysterious and fatal, flowed the river. It had the terrible deliberation and the relentlessness of destiny. (p. 73)

He leaned against the rail and looked at the softly flowing water. (p. 88)

"Would you like me to come to the mouth of the river with you?"
"Oh, I think it would be better if we said good-bye here." (p. 89)

The darkness thinned away and the river was ghostly. (p. 89)

The dawn now was creeping along the river mistily, but the night lurked still in the dark trees of the jungle. (p. 90).

George Orwell
"Shooting an Elephant" (1936)

Interpretation and Background Information

George Orwell's "Shooting an Elephant"

"Shooting an Elephant" was first published in the journal *New Writing* in 1936 and was collected in *Shooting an Elephant and Other Essays* (1950). The story is largely autobiographical.

Short Interpretation of "Shooting an Elephant"

"Shooting an Elephant" presents a psychological study of the effects imperialism can have on the individuals involved. The narrative offers insight into the psyche of a British police officer representing an empire he dislikes. The Western official is confronted with hostility and aggression against not only himself personally but everyone representing the British colonial empire and what it stands for. The colonized reject being dominated by the oppressors and pay them back with disrespect and hatred. These tensions between the colonizer and the colonized are portrayed in the story by Orwell as he reflects back on an incident when he was a police officer in Burma where, as the narrator puts it, "I was hated by large numbers of people – the only time in my life that I have been important enough for this to happen" (p. 94, l. 2-3). The reader should note the irony in the words "important enough" and be prepared for Orwell's irony to deepen and darken throughout the piece.

Wiser now than when the events in the story occurred, the narrator can look back on the incident and criticize his behaviour, at least up to a point. "I was young and ill-educated and I had had to think out my problems in the utter silence that is imposed on every Englishman in the East" (p. 95, l. 10-11). Even in an essay with a message as clear as this one, Orwell prefers to leave his narrator flawed, a technique that allows the reader to both sympathize with his situation and critique his behaviour. Analysing his own situation the narrator explains: "I was stuck between my hatred of the empire I served and my rage against the evil-spirited little beasts who tried to make my job impossible" (p. 95, l. 14-16). The narrator seems to be torn between two positions: his role as a representative of the Brtiish Empire and his personal feelings. Though he is well aware that his anger and disgust at the "natives" ("evil-spirited" and "beasts" he calls them) is a product of colonialism, he still can't help but be tainted by the role he has to play.

The shooting of the elephant is announced as something "which in a roundabout way was enlightening" (p. 96, l. 5-6), something that will offer a "glimpse (…) of the real nature of imperialism" (p. 96, l. 7). Unwilling to shoot the elephant but feeling the pressure to conform to what is expected of a "sahib," the police officer does not have the courage to stand up against the forces of colonialism, whose effects are too complex for him to fully understand, at least not at this time when, "I was young and ill-educated". Under the watchful eyes of two thousand or more Burmese, he feels the pressure to act as they and his fellow Englishmen in the colonial service expect him to act. "I perceived in this moment that when the white man turns tyrant it is his own freedom that he destroys. He becomes a sort of hollow, posing dummy, the conventionalized figure of a sahib. For it is the conditon of his rule that he shall spend his life in trying to impress the 'natives' and so in every crisis he has got to do what the 'natives' expect of him. He wears a mask, and his face grows to fit it" (p. 101, l.1–7).

The fact that he is torn between two positions, his personal attitude and his official role, is further complicated by what the Burmese expect of him. (Most of the onlookers are waiting for the elephant to be shot so they can strip off its meat ("they wanted the meat" (p. 99, l. 12).)

Orwell saves his strongest writing to describe the slow death of the elephant. "You could see the agony of it jolt his whole body and knock the last remnant of strength from his legs. But in falling he seemed for a moment to rise, for as his hind legs collapsed beneath him he seemed to tower upward like a huge rock toppling, his trunk reaching skyward like a tree. He trumpeted for the first and only time. And then down he came, his belly toward me, with a crash that seemed to shake the ground even where I lay" (p. 104 l. 1–7). The similes from nature ("like a huge rock", "his trunk reaching skyward like a tree") only deepen the narrator's crime; by killing the elephant, the similes suggest, he has committed a sacrilege against nature itself. Even the earth is shaken by the animal's death.

The dying elephant has become a symbol for the failure and the near collapse of the British Empire represented by the police officer who acts to fit a "mask" rather than being true to what he knows is right. In the essay's last line – "I often wondered whether any of the others grasped that I had done it solely to avoid looking a fool" (p. 105, l. 14–16) – Orwell, by exposing the flaws in his younger self, exposes the deep-seated effects of colonialism on the colonizers as well as the colonized.

Narrator/Point of View

Orwell published "Shooting an Elephant" as an autobiographical essay and never as a work of fiction, but he employs several fictional techniques to make his points. A good writer of narrative, whether fiction or nonfiction, knows that it's best not put the narrator in too good of a light. By showing how he cannot do the right thing (i.e., not shoot the elephant), Orwell makes it possible for us to understand the effects of imperialism in Burma better than if he had simply written an essay stating his beliefs. The narrator is torn between two positions, his personal and his official role. "Theoretically – and secretly, of course – I was all for the Burmese and all against their oppressors, the British." (p. 95, l. 1–2). But theory isn't action, and his actions prove how deep the corruption of colonialism runs. His official role is to represent the country of oppressors. The narrator gives a detailed insight into various incidents which have resulted in his "rage" (p. 95, l. 15) against the Burmese. Being categorically hated as a representative of the Empire, he adopts a position of an official not responsible for his actions, as they are only the logical result of the imperialist's position expected of him, explaining that "a sahib has got to act like a sahib" (p. 101, l. 9).

The narrator describes himself as an "absurd puppet pushed to and fro by the will of the yellow faces behind" (p. 100, l. 29f). While he has a picture of the Burmese already made up in his mind, always looking for proof to verify his assumptions, the Burmese also have an image of the British representative which has to be filled. Orwell's irony here is clear: if you put on the mask of the colonial oppressor, you will become one. Orwell describes the death of the elephant in detail in order for us to experience the horror of what the narrator has done. And in the end he aims his strongest critique at himself: "I often wondered whether any of the others grasped that I had done it solely to avoid looking a fool" (p. 105, l. 14–16).

Background Information: Edward Said's Orientalism

The literary theorist Edward Said became famous when he coined the phrase "Orientalism" to describe Western attitudes towards the East. His theory is based on the assumption that the idea of the "Orient" is a product of Western thinking which is not based on reality but on the concept of "the Other". The Orient exists only for the West. This concept is constructed by the West, defined by its relation to it and used for political purposes by its representatives. As a negative mirror image of the West the "Orient" is regarded as inferior and alien to the West. The political domination of the East by Western cultures lead to this perception and has strongly influenced writers and thinkers who are part of the formerly dominant culture.

According to Said, the concept of "the Other", the people in the East as the negative pattern of the Westerner, is the basis for imperialist behaviour stressing differences rather than finding correspondences and similarities and helping the imperialists to create a clearly distinguished self-image. Even the most sympathetic Westerners writing about the East are influenced by this "knowledge" of the East, marking it as a counterpoint to Western civilisation and culture and thus adding to a stereotypical image of the East.

Teaching Suggestions

Pre-Reading Activities

1. **Visual prompt**
   Look at the picture of the Indian elephant and write down the things that the picture makes you think of. Now discuss in a small group what kind of associations you had and organise them in a mind map.

2. **In a large crowd**
   Have you ever been in a large crowd when you had to follow the masses (e.g. a concert, football match etc.)? How did you feel?
   You could recreate the feeling. Put the tables and chairs aside. Agree on a direction into which you want to move and start moving slowly. Reflect on the situation afterwards: How did it feel being part of the group and moving along with it?

3. **Shooting an animal?**
   What are your feelings about killing animals? Discuss with your partner.

While-Reading Activities

1. **p. 94 ll. 1–3**
   What associations does the opening sentence evoke? What do you imagine the main character to be like?

2. **p. 96 ll. 5–8**
   The narrator talks about motives for which a despotic government acts. What motives can you think of?

3. **p. 102 ll. 3–21**
   The police officer is ready to act. What do you expect to happen?

After-Reading Activities

1. **Good angel/bad angel**
   The narrator is torn between shooting and not shooting the elephant. Imagine you are an angel/devil whispering in his ear. What would you tell him? Find arguments in the text (cf. copymaster on p. 40).

2. "Afterwards, of course, there were endless discussions about the shooting of the elephant." (p. 105)
   What were the arguments for and against the killing? Prepare a list of arguments for one of the positions and discuss in class.

3. "And my whole life … was a long struggle not to be laughed at." (p. 101)
   Why should the narrator fear to be laughed at? Discuss.

4. **"In order to rule over barbarians you have got to become a barbarian yourself." (George Orwell)**
   Do you agree? Why/ Why not?

5. **"Orientalism was ultimately a political vision of reality whose structure promoted the difference between the familiar (Europe, West, "us") and the strange (the Orient, the East, "them")." (Edward Said)**
   Do you think the narrator is determined in his actions by "Orientalism"? Give reasons for your opinion.

Creative Writing

1. **Writing a dialogue**
   a) Reread the passage where the police officer walks down to the paddy field followed by the people of the village. (p. 99 l. 3 → p. 100 l. 21)
   b) Imagine you are a woman or man in the crowd.
   c) Work with a partner and write a dialogue between two people in the crowd discussing or commenting on the things happening.

2. **Writing a diary entry**
   a) Imagine you had followed the events during the day e.g. as the Burmese subinspector or one of the Indian constables.
   b) Write a diary entry for him giving an insight into his feelings towards the crowd and the British police officer.

3. **Reacting to a Telegraph**
   The following telegraph was sent to Britain in the night after the shooting.

```
++++INCIDENT IN THE COLONIES++STOP+

+++++MOULMEIN, LOWER BURMA++STOP+++

++BRITISH POLICE OFFICER SAVES

THOUSANDS BY KILLING A RAVAGING

ELEPHANT+++STOP+++++++++++
```

Imagine the police officer came back after the event and was invited to a dinner where he talks to someone who had read the telegraph.
He could be talking to a society lady who is impressed by his heroism, a close friend or an official in the police head department.
Write the dialogue between the two.

Composition

1. Reread the passage from the beginning (p. 94 l. 1 → p. 96 l. 4).
   What kind of information about the main character is given?
   What effect does this have on the reader?
   How does it foreshadow what is going to happen?

2. The narrator refers to the Burmese people as "yellow faces above the garish clothes" (p. 100).
   Find other descriptions of the people and their attitudes in the text.
   Which viewpoint does the narrator have?
   How does this account for his behaviour?

3. The narrator gives a detailed description of the man killed by the elephant (p. 98 ll. 2–15).
   What kind of language is used to describe the dead man?
   Why do you think the passage is relevant and comparatively long in retrospective?

4. "I had halted on the road. As soon as I saw the elephant I knew with perfect certainty that I ought not to shoot him." (p. 100 ll. 3–4)
   Read the two following passages (→ p. 101 l. 14).
   What makes the narrator change his mind?
   How does he try to justify his behaviour?

5. According to Edgar Alan Poe (1809–1849) every word in a short story should contribute to its central effect.
   What is the central effect in this story?
   How is Poe's demand fulfilled in Orwell's short story?

Topics for Presentations

1. **Give a short insight into the history of Burma and its political situation today.**
   http://news.bbc.co.uk/2/hi/asia-pacific/country_profiles/1300003.stm

2. **Find out more about the life of George Orwell and inform the class about him.**
   http://www.bbc.co.uk/history/society_culture/art/orwell_01.shtml

3. **Read more about elephants.**
   http://www.bbc.co.uk/nature/wildfacts/factfiles/178.shtml

4. **Find out more about Edward Said and his idea of Orientalism.**
   http://www.postcolonialweb.org/poldiscourse/themes/3.html

Don't shoot the elephant!	Shoot the elephant!

Doris Lessing
"The Second Hut" (1936)

Interpretation and Background Information

Doris Lessing's "The Second Hut"

One of several stories by Lessing that take place in Africa, specifically Southern Rhodesia (now Zimbabwe), "The Second Hut" shows the effects of colonialism on Major Carruthers, once a British soldier, now trying to make it as a farmer. The relationship between three character sets (British, Afrikaans, native) form the dramatic constellation of this somewhat schematic work.

Brief Summary of "The Second Hut"

Major Carruthers, a British farmer in Southern Rhodesia in the early 1930s, has several problems on his hands: his wife is not well, his farm is failing, he's in debt to his brother back in England. But things are not going to get better, as Lessing's opening indicates: "Before that season and his wife's illness, he had thought things could get no worse" (p. 107). What instigates the turn for the worse is his hiring Van Heerden, an Afrikaner, as his foreman. Carruthers gives his new assistant a small hut to live in, only to find out that Van Heerden has moved into it with his nine children and slatternly wife. Angry at being tricked but also repelled by the squalid living conditions of Van Heerden's family, Carruthers becomes "haunted" by them, "he even dreamed of them; and he could not determine whether it was his own or the Dutchman's children who filled his sleep with fear" (p. 124). He also sees that his "bossboy," the native in charge of his other native workers, is not at all pleased with having an Afrikaner working on the farm. Still, he orders that they build for Van Heerden a second hut. "I'm not having any nonsense. If that hut isn't built, there'll be trouble" (p. 129). Obviously unsuited for the job of overseeing a farm in Africa, Major Carruthers is unable to help anyone on his farm. The extent of his impotence is reflected in what he tells Van Heerden after wanting to dismiss him, but then deciding to keep him on: "Remember, I'm not responsible" (p. 123). Even after Carruthers stops Van Heerden hitting the natives, he orders them to keep working on the new hut. On the first night after the family has moved into the second hut, the natives burn it down and Van Heerden's wife loses her youngest child. Though Carruthers tells his bossboy that the hut "must be rebuilt at once" (p. 142), he is "frightened, not so much at his rage, but his humiliation and guilt. He had foreseen it! He had foreseen it all!" (p. 143). The day after the fire, Carruthers returns to Van Heerden where he finds him waiting to deliver his wife's next child, who is coming a month early. Another child? "The idea had not entered [Carruthers'] head; it had been a complete failure of the imagination. If nine children, why not ten? Why not fifteen, for that matter, or twenty? Of course there would be more children. [. . .] He felt weak" (p. 145). Understanding that he's now at the end of his options, Carruthers sees Van Heerden as the representative voice for the continent and he imagines Van Heerden saying to him: "this grey country of poverty that you fear so much, will take on a different look when you actually enter it. You will cease to exist; there is no energy left, when one is wrestling naked with life, for your kind of fine feelings and scruples and regrets" (p. 145). Carruthers returns home and writes the letter his wife has wanted him to write for a long time, asking his brother for a job back in England, even though "each slow difficult word was a nail in the coffin of his pride as a man" p. 146). It's his inability to help anyone in Africa – the natives, his family and himself, Van Heerden and his family – that triggers his admission of failure and his decision to return to England.

A Constellation of Characters

In "The Second Hut" Lessing plays two dominant sets of characters off one another (British and Afrikaans), and uses a (minor) third set (native) as the fulcrum or peripeteia to turn the plot.

I. British and Afrikaans

Lessing parallels Carruthers and his family to that of Van Heerden and his. By placing the description of the two principles – protagonist (Carruthers)/antagonist (Van Heerden) – side by side, we can see how, in part, Lessing establishes the story's conflicts and themes. First, Major Carruthers:

> Even in his appearance, square, close-bitten, disciplined, there had been a hint of softness, or of strain, showing itself in his smile, which was too quick, like the smile of a deaf person afraid of showing incomprehension, and in the anxious look of his eyes. After he left the army he quickly slackened into an almost slovenly carelessness of dress and carriage. Now, in his farm clothes there was nothing left to suggest the soldier. With a loose, stained felt hat on the back of his head, khaki shorts a little too long and too wide, sleeves flapping over spare brown arms, his wispy moustache hiding a strained, set mouth, Major Carruthers looked what he was, a gentleman going to seed." (p. 107–108)

(It's worth noting here, as an example of Lessing's eye for the precise, telling detail, the images in this description, e.g. the "khaki shorts a little too long and too wide". The visual detail actualizes the character in ways an idea – e.g. he was a sad, pathetic man – never could.)

Our first description of Carruthers's antagonist (or dark mirror) Van Heerden is from Carruthers's point of view:

> . . . young, thirty perhaps, sturdily built, with enormous strength in the thick arms and shoulders. His skin was burnt a healthy orange-brown colour. His close hair, smooth as the fur of an animal, reflected no light. His obtuse, generous features were set in a round face, and the eyes were pale grey, nearly colourless. [. . .] It was not that he disliked him for [being an Afrikaner], although his father had been killed in the Boer War, but he had never had anything to do with the Afrikaans people, and his knowledge of them was hearsay, from the Englishmen who had the old prejudice. (p. 113–114)

Immediately following Carruthers' first impressions of Van Heerden, Lessing shifts point of view (surprisingly, since it's the only time she will do so) from the farmer to the Afrikaner: "As for Van Heerden, he immediately recognized [in Carruthers] his traditional enemy, and his inherited dislike was strong. For a moment he appeared obstinate and wary. But they needed each other too badly to nurse old hatreds" (p. 114). Thus the two antagonists are made equal, at least for the moment, the one with his *old prejudice*, the other with his *old hatreds*. The difference between the British ex-soldier and the Afrikaner is bluntly shown when they first enter the hut Carruthers is willing to let Van Heerden live in, and Van Heerden, upon seeing a spider web, "did what Major

Carruthers would have died rather than do: he tore the web across with his bare hands, [then] crushed the spider between his fingers" (p. 106). And of course, Van Heerden, unlike Carruthers, has a "sure understanding of animals" (p. 121). At one point, Lessing pairs the two off, bringing their differences into sharp relief: "The two men faced each other, Major Carruthers tall, flyaway, shambling, bent with responsibility; Van Heerden stiff and defiant" (p. 121–122).

Lessing also juxtaposes the two wives:

> The doctor said it was her heart; and Major Carruthers knew this was true: she had broken down through heart-break over the conditions they lived in. She did not want to get better. The harsh light from outside was shut out with dark blinds, and she turned her face to the wall and lay there, hour after hour, inert and uncomplaining, in a stoicism of defeat nothing could penetrate. Even the children hardly moved her. It was as if she had said to herself: "If I cannot have what I wanted for them, then I wash my hands of life." (p.109)

This pale being wasting away from loss of her previous way of life, once had been a

> pleasant conventional pretty English girl [. . .] bred to make a perfect wife for the professional soldier she had imagined him to be, but chance had wrenched her on to this isolated African farm, into a life which she submitted herself to, as if it had nothing to do with her. [. . .] As the house grew shabby, and the furniture, and her clothes could not be replaced; when she looked into the mirror and saw her drying, untidy hair and roughening face, she would give a quick high laugh and say, "Dear me, the things one comes to!" (p. 109)

Van Heerden's wife, on the other hand, is a "vast slatternly woman" holding, when we first see her, a pot over a fire. In her fecundity (nine children with another about to be born), "She reminded [Carruthers] of a sow among her litter" (p. 119). Her nine children, "each as tow-headed as the first, with that bleached sapless look common to white children in the tropics who have been subjected to too much sun" (p. 119) and whom the father keeps out of school, are put in contrast to Carruthers's two sons at boarding school, who "were pale, fine-drawn creatures, almost transparent-looking in their thin nervous fairness, with the defensive and wary manners of the young who have been brought up to expect a better way of life than they enjoy. Their anxious solicitude wore on Major Carruthers' already over-sensitized nerves" (p. 110).

II. Native

A third character group consisting of the bossboy and the other native workers is kept in the background for both narrative and thematic effect. Without the entry of the natives into the story, the stalemate between Carruthers and Van Heerden would not be broken. The natives serve as the story's fulcrum, the instigators of the reversal or peripeteia. "'Dutchmen are no good,' said the bossboy simply, voicing the hatred of the black man for that section of the white people he considers his most brutal oppressors" (p.125), establishing the cultural conflict at the story's base. When we hear that Van Heerden treats the natives "like dogs", a "continual friction" (p. 124) is now established on the farm.

The natives are also used for the turn (for the worse) at the story's midpoint when Carruthers decides that all the work around the farm has to wait for the second hut to be built (p. 128). The plot climaxes around Carruthers seeing Van Heerden abusing the workers. "Van Heerden using his open palms in a series of quick swinging slaps against [the native workers'] faces, knocking them sideways against each other: it was as if he were cuffing his own children in a fit of anger" (p. 136). Caught between not wanting his workers to be abused by Van Heerden and wanting to come to his fellow white man's aid, the dithering Britisher's problems appear even more unsolvable.

We do not see the natives as fully portrayed as the Major and his Afrikaans assistant, not because of any lack in Lessing's skills, but perhaps because they are in the background for the foreign Carruthers who feels a closer affinity to (and dismay at) Van Heerden than to them. After he enters the hut and sees that Van Heerden has a large family living there, Carruthers is angry that he's been duped by the Afrikaner, but then his feelings become more mixed. "His anger was now mingled with the shamed discomfort of trying to imagine what it must be like to live in such squalor" (p. 120). How the natives live in the bush, however, stays outside his consciousness. The Africa of the natives remains remote but ever present in the story.

A Four-roomed Shack and Two Huts

"The Second Hut" offers us another signifying cluster, this time of the story's principle dwellings, which, like the people that live in them, also may be usefully contrasted and compared.

The house where Carruthers and his wife live

> had that brave, worn appearance of those struggling to keep up appearances. It was a four-roomed shack, its red roof dulling to streaky brown. It was the sort of house an apprentice farmer builds as a temporary shelter till he can afford better. Inside, good but battered furniture stood over worn places in the rugs; the piano was out of tune and the notes stuck; the silver tea things from the big narrow house in England where his brother (a lawyer) now lived were used as ornaments, and inside were bits of paper, accounts, rubber, old corks. (p. 108)

This house, more a run-down "four-roomed shack," a poor and distant relative of the British house of the wife's expectations, is contrasted to the dung-floored, insect-ridden, "black foetid hut" (p. 120) Carruthers allows Van Heerden to inhabit:

> The thatched hut stood in the uncleared bush. Grass grew to the walls and reached up to meet the slanting thatch. Trees mingled their branches overhead. It was round, built of poles and mud and with a stamped dung floor. Inside there was a stale musty smell because of the ants and beetles that had been at the sacks of grain. The one window was boarded over, and it was quite dark. In the confusing shafts of light from the door, a thick sheet of felted spider web showed itself, like a curtain halving the interior, as full of small flies and insects as a butcher-bird's cache. (p. 116)

Were the opposition between Carruthers and Van Heerden a fruitful one, a worthy third abode might dialectically arise. Instead, the second hut Carruthers forces the natives to build for the Dutchman, is burnt to the ground. In her description of the burning, Lessing personifies the hut. "Its frail skeleton was still erect, but twisting and writhing incandescently within its envelop of flame, and it collapsed slowly as he came up, subsiding in a crash of sparks" (p. 140). That the personification of the hut stands uncomfortably beside the burning death of the Van Heerdens' youngest child only deepens the horror.

Lessing's Style

If some students find Lessing's prose uneven or a bit clumsy or stale, that's because it sometimes is. In the story's penultimate paragraph, Lessing finds the right language and imagery to connect Carruthers to his wife again and show the possibility of hope for a new life back in England: "'I've written for a job at Home,' he said simply, laying his hand on her thin dry wrist, and feeling the slow pulse beat up suddenly against his palm" (p. 146). The language is precise, clear, musical ("feeling the slow pulse beat up") and sensual ("her thin dry wrist"; her pulse beating "against his palm"). Alas, this isn't the ending; Lessing's offers one more paragraph, where the language fails to freshen the sentimentality inherent in the moment: "He watched curiously as her face crumpled and the tears of thankfulness and release ran slowly down her cheeks and soaked the pillow" (p. 146). We even wonder why he watches "curiously," since her behavior is what we expect from her character; even for someone as slow to comprehend as Carruthers, the adverb is not entirely credible.

We can find another example of clumsiness in the opening sentence where, after the colon, we read: "until then, poverty had meant not to deviate further than snapping point from what he had been brought up to think of as a normal life" (p. 107). We can understand what she means, that for him poverty begins when he starts to lose what constitutes for him a normal life, but "not to deviate further than snapping point" is not exactly the clearest image. Still, in its awkwardness, or specialness (*snapping point*), one finds part of Lessing's power as a writer. Her principle strengths, in addition to her eye for the precise, telling detail (as noted earlier), can be found in her concepts (cf. her novella *The Fifth Child*), her charged imagery (e.g. "the black foetid hut and the pathetic futureless children" [p. 120]), the accuracy of her critique regarding racial, gender, and political issues, and her skill at making plot adhere to character.

Background Information: The Elements of Plot

Plot, we should remember, is the author's arrangement of the events in a story and need not be chronological; *story*, on the other hand, is closer to a history of the events, both before [i.e. the *backstory*] and after the narrative ends.

In Aristotelian terms, plots are propelled by *conflict* that, along with various *complications*, give rise (*rising action*) to further complications and a deepening of conflict, until at a crisis point or *climax* (approximately two-thirds through the story), a turn or *peripeteia* occurs, instigating the plot's *reversal* or *falling action*, *recognition* and *resolution*. (Sophocles's *Oedipus Rex* served as Aristotle's central structural model.)

In his *Poetics*, Aristotle defines reversal as "a change by which the action veers round to its opposite"(*Poetics*, tr. S. H. Butcher). Recognition "is a change from ignorance to knowledge, producing" an emotional change in a character. "Recognition, then, being between persons, it may happen that one person only is recognized by the other – when the latter is already known – or it may be necessary that the recognition should be on both sides." (Which is it in "The Second Hut"? The bossboy and Van Heerden, even his sickly wife, already recognize

Carruthers, as much as they likely ever will; Carruthers is the protagonist who is granted recognition.)

For Aristotle, the structure of the plot should arise out of the characters; who and what the characters are establishes what happens. "It is therefore evident that the unraveling of the plot, no less than the complication, must arise out of the plot itself, it must not be brought about by the *Deus ex Machina* – as in the *Medea*, or in the return of the Greeks in the *Iliad*." As a consequence, the best recognition "arises from the incidents themselves". (Carruthers's inability to mediate between the natives and the Afrikaners is what, in part, both leads to and is his recognition.)

Teaching Suggestions

Pre-Reading Activities

1. Draw a chart of what you understand as a story's plot. Compare the charts and discuss the elements of plot.

2. Have the students pick a country of their choice for them to imagine moving to. What problems would they have trying to start a new life elsewhere? What job do they think they would have?

While-Reading Activity

Draw a plot chart of "The Second Hut," noting the major plot points. (You might want to use as your model an arch, with the rising curve leading to the climax (rounded, not pointed, since climaxes occur over a period of time, i.e. they are events lived through by the characters as well as the reader), then the downward curve leading to the dénouement.

After-Reading Activities / Analysis

1. For Aristotle plot arises out of character. Discuss the ways this is true of "The Second Hut." How do the characters, specifically Major Carruthers, drive the action, bring about the events that form the story's plot? (See "Background Information: The Elements of Plot" above.)

2. Lessing uses the second hut both as the story's title and object of contention between the various sets of characters. Discuss its significance, in part by examining closely the descriptions of the first hut (p. 115–116, 119–120 and 130–131) and the "death" of the second hut (p. 139–140). (See above "A Four-roomed Shack and Two Huts".)

Topics for Class Discussion

1. Discuss the story's three basic character sets – British, Afrikaners, native – and the characters associated with each group. Where do they parallel? How does the constellation of this set generate the story's plot? (See "A Constellation of Characters" and "Background Information: The Elements of Plot" above.)

2. Find a passage in which the language seems particularly powerful to you, then one in which the language seems less strong or fresh or inadequate to the story's demands. Discuss your choices without using "because I like it/don't like it" as your reason. (See above section on "Lessing's Style".)

Creative Writing

You live in a hut, a second hut. Someone with a bigger hut, perhaps even a house, is whom you work for. You are the mother or the father. Several children live in the hut with you. You are poor, you are cold, you are hungry. You love your children. You love your husband/wife. – With these as your criteria, write a monologue about your life. (Use specific details and language that engages all five senses.)

Composition

1. According to Caroline Gordon and Allen Tate in their anthology House of Fiction, "[a]s in life, it is the event which is at once perfectly probable and yet unforeseeable which precipitates or give its final direction to the action." What event in "The Second Hut" fits these criteria? Justify your choice.

2. Why does Lessing portray Major Carruthers as a weak man ("a hint of softness" about him, with a smile "too quick, like the smile of a deaf person afraid of showing incomprehension" [p. 107]). What does the story gain by this choice?

3. Compare and contrast the story's three "houses" – the four-roomed shack, the first hut, the second hut. What do each tell us about the characters? Support your answer by closely examining Lessing's descriptions of the buildings.

Topics for Presentations

1. **Give a short report on Lessing's career.**
   Klein, Carole: *Doris Lessing: A Biography.* New York: Carroll & Graf, 2000.
   McLeod, John: *Postcolonial London: Rewriting the Metropolis.* London: Routledge, 2004.
   Cheng, Yuan-Jung: *Heralds of the Postmodern: Madness and Fiction in Conrad, Wolf, and Lessing.* New York; Frankfurt am Main; Berlin: Lang, 1999.
   Kugler-Euerle, Gabriele: *Geschlechtsspezifik und Englischunterricht: Studien zur Literaturdidaktik und Rezeption literarischer Texte am Beispiel Doris Lessings.* Trier: WVT, Wiss. Verl. Trier, 1998. Zugl.: Koblenz, Landau, Univ., Diss., 1996
   Saxton, Ruth, ed.: *Woolf and Lessing: Breaking the Mold.* Basingstoke: Macmillan, 1994.
   Biographical Links:
   British Arts Council: http://www.contemporarywriters.com/authors/?p=auth60
   http://www.kirjasto.sci.fi/dlessing.htm
   http://lessing.redmood.com/biography.html
   http://en.wikipedia.org/wiki/Doris_Lessing

2. **Give a short report on Lessing's years in Africa.**
   See in particular the first volume of Lessing's autobiography, *Under My Skin: Volume I of My Autobiography, to 1949.* HarperCollins, 1994 (birth to end of S. Africa years)
   Lessing, Doris: *Walking in the Shade: Volume II of My Autobiography 1949–1962.* HarperCollins, 1997.

3. **Give a presentation of the history of Southern Rhodesia.**
   Mears, Chris: *Goodbye Rhodesia.* Antony Rowe Publishing Services, 2005.
   Leys, Colin: *European Politics in Southern Rhodesia.* Greenwood Press, 1982.
   Keppel-Jones, Arthur: *Rhodes and Rhodesia: The White Conquest of Zimbabwe, 1884–1902.* McGill-Queen's University Press, 1996.

4. **Give a presentation on Afrikaans and Afrikaners.**
   Patterson, Sheila: *The Last Trek: A Study of the Boer People and the Afrikaner Nation* (Routledge Library Editions: Anthropology & Ethnography). Routledge, an imprint of Taylor & Francis Books Ltd, 2004.
   Ponelis, Friedrich Albert: *The Development of Afrikaans* (Duisburg Papers on Research in Language & Culture). Peter Lang Publishing Inc, US, 1993.

5. **Report on the current condition of Zimbabwe.**
   Hill, Geoff: *What Happens After Mugabe?: Can Zimbabwe Rise From the Ashes.* Zebra Press, 2005.
   Moore, Donald S.: *Suffering for Territory: Race, Place, and Power in Zimbabwe.* Duke University Press, 2005.
   Lessing, Doris: *African Laughter: Four Visits to Zimbabwe.* Flamingo, 1993.
   Sheers, Owen: *The Dust Diaries.* London: Faber and Faber, 2005.
   http://en.wikipedia.org/wiki/Southern_Rhodesia
   http://en.wikipedia.org/wiki/Rhodesia

6. **Give a plot summary of Sophocles's *Oedipus Rex* and its importance to the basic elements of plot as Aristotle delineates them in the Poetics.**

Chinua Achebe
"Dead Men's Path" (1953)

Interpretation and Background Information

Chinua Achebe's "Dead Men's Path"

A story about the power and importance of tradition, "Dead Men's Path" partakes of both the old and new in its themes and its telling. Its implications for today's readers are as disturbing as they are enlightening.

Short Summary and Interpretation of "Dead Men's Path"

In 1949 in a fictitious African country (the reader can assume, with little guilt, that Ndume is a stand-in for Achebe's homeland Nigeria), an "energetic" young man named Michael Obi and his wife Nancy move to a village where he takes on the position of headmaster of a mission school. The previous headmaster was one of those narrow-minded, "older and often less-educated" (p. 149) types of educators. Michael is looking forward to overturning the old ways. He dedicates himself to his job; his wife concentrates on turning the school compound into a flower garden. A week before an official inspector is to arrive to assess how the new headmaster is getting along, an old woman tramples through the garden where once an ancestral footpath ran. Obi is outraged ("scandalized" the text has it) by the desecration of Nancy's garden when he sees the woman "hobble right across the compound, through a marigold flower-bed and the hedges" (p. 151). Then, even though he has been told by a teacher who has been at the school for three years that the footpath "connects the village shrine with their place of burial and that "a big row" once occurred "when we attempted to close it" (p. 152), Obi, fearing what the Government Education Officer will think when he comes to inspect the school, has sticks planted across the path "where it entered and left the school premises. These were further strengthened with barbed wire" (p. 152). The priest of the village visits Obi and politely tells him of the importance of the path to both the living and the dead. "But most important," the old man says, "it is the path of children coming in to be born . . ." Our "hero", smugly, condescendingly, "listened with a satisfied smile", then replies that his job "is to eradicate just such beliefs as that" (p. 153). When two days after the priest's visit a young woman dies in childbirth, "heavy sacrifices" are "prescribed" by a diviner. Obi wakes "up the next morning among the ruins of his work." The garden has been torn up, "the flowers trampled to death and one of the school buildings pulled down . . ."The final sentence informs us that "the white Supervisor came to inspect the school and wrote a nasty report" about the new headmaster who has brought on a "tribal-war situation" (p. 154) between the mission school and the villagers.

"Dead Men's Path" is a somewhat dissonant mix of the old and the new. Within the story's simple structure, derived from the oral folk tale tradition, the contemporary details seem out of place. ("'A penny for your thoughts, Mike,' said Nancy [...] imitating the woman's magazine she read" (p. 151).) Since "Dead Men's Path" insists we respect the past and uses a form from the past (the tale) to deliver this message, it's no surprise that the new is what lies in ruins at the tale's end.

There are in fact few if any surprises in the story. From the first paragraph, Achebe telegraphs the plot and the theme. The few details we have about Michael and Nancy Obi suggest their naiveté and shallowness. More stereotype than character, Michael is the eager-beaver kind of educator, dedicated to his mission of modernization and willing to ignore or trample on African traditions. Not only is he a fool, he's a tool of the white colonialists, for the mission school is a colonial school and the supervisor who writes up the "nasty report" on Obi is "white" – a detail that Achebe serves up to us only in the story's final sentence.

Designed to deliver a message, "Dead Men's Path" has little need for subtlety in its characterization, language, or narrative development. There are no fully developed scenes; no opportunity is given to experience the story as something lived, something physically held, felt, breathed, sensed in its being. The objective is to move the story along as quickly as possible and have every aspect of it relate to the message that the old beliefs should at the very least be respected. In a sense, then, the old priest, who "tapped on the floor, by way of emphasis, each time he made a new point in his argument" (p. 152), mirrors Achebe who taps or bangs the tale when he wishes to make his points.

Language

"Dead Men's Path" presents two opposing beliefs, one represented by the new headmaster, the other by the old priest. The battle lines are clearly drawn: new belief versus old belief. (One cannot say secularism here, since Ndume Central School is a "mission" school.) To get his point across in such a *short* tale, Achebe must use words that clearly mark out the differences between the two views.

The dichotomy is established in the first paragraph: "young" headmaster versus "older and less-educated" previous headmasters. The story's two central symbols – ancestral footpath, the flower garden – are also opposed. Nancy's new flower garden is no match for the old footpath, which has a deep past and a direct link (it *is* the link) to the supernatural.

In the words associated with the new headmaster and the old priest, Achebe emphasizes the dichotomies of new/old, modern/traditional, shallow/deep. In the story's beginning, when he *condemns* the *narrow*, *less-educated* headmasters, we see him as a harsh, perhaps unfeeling and unimaginative critic of traditional belief. Obi's *condemnation infects* his wife, who also develops a *passion* for the *modern methods* and *denigrates* the *old and superannuated*. Regarding the author's depiction of Nancy, it's no random matter that the only thing we hear straight from her mouth is a cliché of the most vacuous, inane, and imitative sort derived from a "woman's magazine": "'A penny for your thoughts, Mike,' said Nancy [...] imitating the woman's magazine she read" (p. 151).

The headmaster exhibits the same narrow-mindedness and rigid moralism of his predecessors when he's *scandalized* by the old woman's trampling the garden. His reaction is to deny access to the past, to drive in stakes and erect a *barbed wire* barrier, reminding us immediately of other horrors perpetuated by colonialist, racists and ideologues the world over.

Achebe uses parallelism to establish both the similarity and subtle difference between Obi and the priest. Obi is *stoop-shouldered* and *frail*, whereas the old priest has a *slight stoop* and a *stout walking-stick* which he quietly but powerfully taps to make his points. Whereas Obi speaks of the *whole purpose* and the *whole idea*, the priest speaks of *whole life*. The author juxtaposes the priest's politeness (*what you say may be true*), serious demeanor, and wisdom (the aphorism about the hawk and eagle) to the mockery and smugness of the new headmaster with his *satisfied smile*. The headmaster speaks of *eradicating* the ideas of the priest who is taking a stand for *our ancestors*, *the practices of our fathers*, and *the path of children coming to be born*.

Ironically, in the end it is the *white* supervisor who labels Obi's *zeal misguided*.

Background Information: Traditional Folk Tale vs. Modern Short Story

At not much over a thousand words, "Dead Men's Path" is more a short-short than a short story. In fact, Achebe himself would likely characterize it as simply a story, i.e., a narrative form more closely linked to the traditional tale than to what we have recognized for not much over a century as the modern short story, with its emphasis on character over type, complexity over simplicity, realism over fantasy, or, say, the study (thought and feeling) over the pulpit (message). Folk tales, at least in their structure, are of the same simple design as Achebe's story, and like the folk tale "Dead Men's Path" gives us two-dimensional types rather than three-dimensional characters. In its length and choice of narrative strategies (lack of fully developed characters or scenes, elliptical leaps), the folk tale is an appropriate form if one wants to emphasize the fantastic or deliver a message. You can't put too much flesh on the skeletal folk tale, but at least you can dress it up with fantastic coloration or drape it with morals. Achebe's story doesn't utilize the fantastic as such, but in its central image – the footpath – it acknowledges the importance of the fantastic, or at least a respect for traditional beliefs. Thus the form Achebe has chosen fits his message, even though the events of the tale are "modern" (1949, the conflict of the new versus the old) and realistic. Everything in the story could have happened and probably more or less did – and still does.

Implications

When the old priest meets with the new headmaster he says, "What I always say is: let the hawk perch and let the eagle perch" (p. 153). The implication is that both birds should be able to live in the same tree, in this case traditional belief in the footpath as a link from the living to the dead and the yet-to-be-born and the new beliefs taught at the school. How is this to be achieved? What compromise could be reached? Perhaps rather than move the footpath the headmaster might move the flowers? But the headmaster isn't interested in compromise, only in how the school will appear to the white (read: colonialist, racist) Supervisor.

By portraying the priest as old, calm, and wise, and associating him with the supernatural, and portraying the headmaster as a young fool eager to trash the past, the reader is left with no room to wiggle and no ambiguity – unless one looks beyond the story's limits and considers that when Tradition (the old beliefs) destroys the New (the school) the destruction is not always to the good. Granted that the school here is seen as "modern" to bad effect and the headmaster more a slave than a master to the white Christian (it is a mission school, after all) colonialists. But still the building is torn down, the grounds are ruined, and if someone had been in that building … Well, barbed wire seems like an extreme measure (of course the barbed wire in a sense imprisons those within the boundary as well as keeps others out) and the diviner prescribes extreme measures in turn. But when we consider how easy it would be in today's world to call the old priest a terrorist, assuming he knew or supported the diviner's advice, the story's message suddenly becomes more mixed.

Teaching Suggestions

Pre-Reading Activities

1. Name some aspects in our society considered traditional. Are they all deserving of respect and worth preserving? Which ones are? Which ones, if any, aren't?

2. Tell the students you have a word problem for them. No, not one of those math word problems, but one that deals with positive and negative values about a person. Then have them imagine that your current headmaster or headmistress is being replaced by a headmaster (to keep to the gender in the story) whom they've heard enough about to make an assessment of whether or not he will be any good at his new post. Half the class supports Headmaster B and assumes he will be good at his new job; this group jots down as many positive adjectives as they can about him in a short period of time. The other half believes the new headmaster will be terrible at his job; this group comes up with negative adjectives about him. Poor Headmaster B. The students share their praising and condemning adjectives, while you assist them with their vocabulary. Then they are told in the story they are about to read, Achebe's "Dead Men's Path", a young man will be assigned as the new headmaster for a mission school in an African country. As they read the story, they may want to note those words that seem to them judgmental in the way their adjectives were.

While-Reading Activity

The students begin to note and consider the purpose and effect of some of the negatively judgmental words associated with Obi (about or used by him) vs. more positive ones that relate to the old priest:

New Headmaster	Old Priest
condemnation	slight stoop
narrow	stout walking-stick
less-educated	tapped
infected	ancestral
denigration	whole life
downcast	our ancestors
misfortune	the path of children … to be born
stoop-shouldered	the practices of our fathers
frail	
backward	
scandalized	
barbed wire	
eradicate	
burdensome	
tramped	
nasty	
misguided	

After-Reading Activities / Analysis

1. **Compare Achebe's description of the old priest to that of Michael Obi. Look closely at the language and the "weighted" words, those that in the context of the story judge the characters and establish their view of life. (See above word list and the section on "Language")**

2. **Have the students look closely again at the first paragraph, imagining this is the first time they have read it. Then, continuing to imagine that the story is utterly fresh to them, that they don't yet know the ending, have them analyze each sentence of the first paragraph in terms of what it suggests for the possible story to come.** It's in a story's opening lines or first paragraph that the author leads us – sometimes gently, sometimes with a kick or shove – into the universe of her tale. Students alert to what's going on in terms of the character, plot, and language at the beginning are more likely to find what follows of greater interest. ("What's going to happen next? What's the next sentence? the next word?") An acquired adeptness at reading beginnings assists in the appreciation of a story's aesthetics and thematic concerns.

   The story begins with the main character's wish granted, an ominous opening, especially if you consider the dictum "Watch out or what you wish for you might get." Wishes fulfilled, especially in the opening line of a short story, often turn to regrets. "Michael Obi's hopes were fulfilled much earlier than he had expected." It's in the "much earlier than he had expected" that the reader should detect the seed of the problem that will come back to haunt Obi. The second sentence names the wish granted – "He was appointed head master" – and delivers the requisite information as to time and place – "of Ndume Central School in January 1949." The third sentence establishes more clearly the conflict: the school, having "always been a nonprogressive" one, decides to hire our "young and energetic man". The reader is now alerted to the fact that there might well be a conflict involved here between the administration of the school (those in power and authority) and the protagonist (the individual). But that's not all: Obi himself must play the role he's been hired for, that is, "a young and energetic man," a kind of savior. Will he succeed or not? Or will the story be more ambiguous and offer us both success and failure? From the outside, as in many stories and fairy tales (for example, Kafka's *Das Schloss*), a character is summoned to solve a problem. How will the outsider be treated? Will he be accepted or ostracized? What problems await him? Other questions come to mind, without the reader even willing them, such as: Will our main character, because of his youth and status as an outsider, suffer because of youth's inherent naiveté? The next sentence suggests the answer to that question will be "Yes." "He had many wonderful ideas and this was an opportunity to put them into practice." Obi is beginning to look like a particular type of fool, the kind whose enthusiasm and optimism are destined if not for demolishing at least for a rough ride. The nature of narrative requires that such enthusiasm be thwarted, if only for a while. Otherwise the story has nowhere to go, no hill of rising action to climb. The next sentence, the paragraph's longest, provides the reader with details about Obi's past, specifically ones dealing with his credentials – "sound secondary school education" designated by the "official records" as a "pivotal teacher" – which "set him apart from the other headmasters in the mission field", emphasizing both his separateness and the success he has become accustomed to, the source of his optimism. The final sentence of the paragraph is the most revealing one about Obi ("He was outspoken in his condemnation of the narrow views of these older and often less-educated ones.") in that it establishes his attitude toward and philosophy of education. To the conflict mix now can be added: Youth vs. Age, Progressive vs. Conservative, and other variants of the New/Old dichotomy.

Achebe has now laid out his tools (irony among them) and built the set (time, place, protagonist, potential conflict) upon which the rest of the story will be performed.

Topics for Class Discussion

1. Have the students search out the "editorial" (judgmental) adjectives in the story and discuss their effectiveness to the story's themes.

2. Compare and contrast the simple narrative structure with its lack of developed scenes and complex characters to other stories in the textbook, e.g. "An Outpost of Progress" or "The Black Madonna".

3. Read to the class an African folk tale or one of Amos Tutuola's fantastic tales and have them compare its narrative methods to those used by Achebe.

Creative Writing

1. Choose the persona of one of the following characters from which to write a brief report on the "tribal-war" situation that occurred at Ndume Central School in 1949: Michael Obi; Nancy Obi; the old priest; the diviner; the white Supervisor; a student at the school.

2. Using Achebe's opening paragraph as your beginning, write your own version by either attempting to develop more fully the scenes and characters as you would find in a so-called modern short story or making up your own tale that turns out differently.

3. After reading or listening to a few African folk tales, write a short folk tale of your own.

Composition

1. Why did Achebe choose to write his story using the narrative form of the folk tale?

2. In his introduction to *African Short Stories* (1984) which he co-edited, Achebe says that his criterion for inclusion in the collection "was ultimately literary merit". Why do you think he used "literary merit" as his main criterion? Do you think the same criterion or some other was applied in selecting this story for *The Many Voices of English*?

3. In what sense was the destruction by the villagers of the school an act of terrorism? In what sense was it not?

Topics for Presentations

1. **Give a short report on the history of Nigeria, considering especially the effects of colonialism on the country in 1949.**
   http://en.wikipedia.org/wiki/Nigeria
   http://en.wikipedia.org/wiki/History_of_Nigeria
   http://www.internews.org/nigeria/history_main.htm
   http://www.britannica.com/ebi/article-229718
   "West Africa and Colonialism, Part 3" by Wendy McElroy: http://www.fff.org/freedom/fd0412f.
   asp
   http://www.bbc.co.uk/worldservice/africa/features/storyofafrica/
   "The history of the continent from an African perspective, from the origins of humankind to the end of South African apartheid" by major African historians (Jacob Ajayi, George Abungu, Director-General of the National Museums of Kenya and others). Includes audio of each segment of the BBC program. (Requires sound card, speaker or headphone). Each segment has a timeline, bibliography, useful links.

2. **In August 2005 National Public Radio's Morning Edition presented a series of reports on the current state of affairs in Nigeria, especially the relations between the oil companies, the government, the citizens, and the environment. Listen to the reports at the NPR website and present a summary of them for the class.**
   Oil Money Divides Nigeria
   http://www.npr.org/templates/story/story.php?storyId=4803867
   Series:
   Gas Flaring Continues to Plague Nigeria (Aug. 25, 2005)
   Corruption Clouds Nigeria's Growing Gas Business (Aug. 26, 2005)
   Deadly Oil Skirmish Scars Nigerian Town (Aug. 25, 2005)
   Navigating Nigeria's Muddy Landscape (Aug. 24, 2005)
   A Rebel or a Thief? One Man's Niger Delta Claim (Aug. 24, 2005)
   Oil Pits Locals Against Companies, Government (Aug. 23, 2005)
   The Race to Share in Nigeria's Oil Bounty (Aug. 22, 2005)

3. **Give a presentation on African folk tales.**
   Eight Zulu Folk Tales:
   http://www.canteach.ca/elementary/africa.html
   Nigerian Stories:
   http://www.motherlandnigeria.com/stories.html

4. **Give short reports on these contemporary Nigerian authors:**
   Chinua Achebe:
   http://www.kirjasto.sci.fi/achebe.htm
   Wole Soyinka:
   http://nobelprize.org/literature/laureates/1986/soyinka-bio.html
   http://www.kirjasto.sci.fi/soyinka.htm
   Amos Tutuola:
   http://www.kirjasto.sci.fi/tutuola.htm

5. **Give a presentation on the importance of openings in a work of fiction.**
   One useful source is *The Story Begins: Essays on Literature* (Harcourt, 1999), in which Amos Oz analyzes the opening sections of novels and short stories by such writers as Agnon, Gogol, Kafka, Chekhov, and García Márquez. He writes about the concept of "beginnings," what the beginning of a novel or short story might "mean" to the author and how important it is, concentrating on opening paragraphs where what the author promises may or may not be delivered later, or delivered in surprising ways.

R. K. Narayan
"A Horse and Two Goats" (1960)

Interpretation and Background Information

R.K. Narayan's "A Horse and Two Goats"

"A Horse and Two Goats" was first published in an Indian newspaper but it was not until 1970 that a collection of short stories called "A Horse and Two Goats" attracted a wider public attention for the title story. Unlike the major novels published by Narayan it is not set in the fictional town called Malgudi which was invented by Narayan and which has since become almost a national myth. The story exists in two versions differing in length and detail. In the preface to *Under the Banyan Tree and Other Stories* (1985) Narayan explains that he had been inspired by an American friend visiting after he had picked up a clay horse at a small village.

Short Interpretation of "A Horse and Two Goats"

Narayan's short story "A Horse and Two Goats" is concerned with two major issues: the clash of Western and Eastern culture and the inability of the two men representing these cultures to communicate because they are limited to their own culturally determined viewpoint and their own language.

The beginning of the story reveals its cinematic quality. Zooming in from the wider range of an atlas to the local survey map where the village is only "indicated by a tiny dot" (p. 156), the reader is taken to the outskirts of a village which seems to be as small and irrelevant to the way of the world as the dot on the map. The opening sequence concentrates on a detailed description of the clay horse which guards the entrance of the village, a persistent symbol of the Hindu culture practiced in the region but now "forgotten and unnoticed" (p. 157).

What seems at first to be an everyday scene of an old man sitting in the shade turns into an event that will change the old man's life completely. Lack of movement, waiting for the usual events to take place, marks the life of the old man. His waiting is interrupted by a station wagon which stops right in front of him. A foreigner dressed in khaki-coloured clothes gets out of the car and starts a conversation with the old man.

This "conversation" is in many ways special. The situation is interpreted differently by the two participants: while the American is looking for the owner of the horse in order to buy it from him, the old man at first takes the tourist for a governmental representative and thus a colonizer. The two men speak each in their native tongue, one Tamil, the other English, neither of which the other understands, thus limiting their communication to non-verbal means such as gestures and facial expressions and making the trade or sale of the statue difficult. This scene of failed communication allows Narayan to develop his comedy and themes.

With his typical humorous style Narayan has his omniscient narrator comment on the "conversation" between the two men. He uses a narrator who explains background information to the reader and gives an insight into the characters and in particular the old man's attitudes. The communication is based on differences, and inter-cultural understanding is only possible in certain aspects. It is particularly in connection with money that the cultural and economic differences become obvious. While the old man has never seen as much money as the American is offering, the amount offered is what the tourist is ready to pay for a statue which does not even have any religious value for him. The clash of cultures could not be more obvious.

The cultural differences become apparent when we look at what the two men talk about. While the American is interested in economic aspects, bargaining and means of transportation for what he wishes to buy, the old man speaks of prophetic visions about Kalki the horse and Vishnu and inquires about the family of the tourist and family life in his country. It might seem that the old man is completely free of financial concerns, but his "dream of a lifetime" (p. 164), of raising goats to sell in order to open a shop is clearly a goal that is also, though perhaps not equally, materialistic. His dream is comparable to the "American dream", hoping to make it from a poor shepherd to a shop owner. The idea of economic success is deeply rooted in him. The American, however, is a man of leisure. He wants to own the statue of the horse and is unaware of its religious meaning and traditional value.

The community of the village has already been influenced by contact with the West regarded as evil by the old man: "The cinema has spoiled the people and taught them how to do evil things." (p. 158). His reaction to the American tourist is marked by his former contacts to Western culture. Limited to his previous experiences, the old man mistakes the American tourist for a police officer. This gives the reader another insight into the feelings of the former colonized towards the Westerners, once their colonizers. However, the American does not represent the colonizing power in an administrative sense but a new force of cultural imperialism. The communicative situation is marked by the old man's feeling of being questioned by a superior, someone in power. Even if he becomes aware of his own misinterpretation when a "financial element was entering their talk" (p. 163), the superiority of the foreigner seems to be carried on. And it is only in the end when the old man leaves that his equality in action becomes obvious. He is familiar with the surroundings, at home with the village's procedures and values and the American is left behind waiting, dependent on the old man's help. The open ending leaves it to the reader to decide what will happen to the two men afterwards.

There is evidence in the text that the American will accomplish his task of buying the horse in the opening sequence: "In proof thereof, he could, until quite recently, point in the direction of a massive guardian at the portals of the village, in the shape of a horse moulded out of clay, baked, burnt, and brightly coloured" (p. 156). This clearly indicates that the horse is no longer where it had been for decades. Further hints can be found in the reaction of the natural surroundings to the American's appearance: "A sudden gust of wind churned up the dust and the dead leaves on the roadside unto a ghostly column and propelled it toward the mountain road." (p. 160). Like the dead leaves and the dust, the horse, long forgotten and not cared for by most of the villagers, will be taken away by the tourist who suddenly appeared like the wind taking the leaves and the dust along the mountain road.

This indicates that one culture, the American, takes control over another by trading in unequal circumstances. If the culture of the American dominates, as the above points suggest (the statue taken and the village infiltrated by Western attitudes and values), then it will gain even more power over the other culture and lead to a loss of symmetry in the exchange. However, the personal benefit for the old man (money to open a store) cannot be disputed.

Narrator/Point of View

The 3rd person narrative gives an insight into both men's attitudes and makes it possible for the reader to follow the lack of communication. The shift from side to side lends the narrative a scenic quality. The style is simple and unadorned but full of references to the religious background of Hinduism. The narrator comments on the limitation of the characters' insights into the other's cultural background: While the old man does not even understand the word "America" because it is not pronounced in a way he is familiar with, the American cannot understand more than the word "avatar" when the old man tells him about the cultural and religious relevance of the horse. Like the American the Western reader of the story is not familiar with the religious background of the statue and does not have the means to follow the old man's explanations. The narrator comments on this lack of understanding in an ironical tone: "At this stage the mutual mystification was complete" (p. 162).

The conversation is mostly given in direct speech (with the old man's words translated into English) with some sequences in free indirect discourse making the reader participate in the old man's feelings and thoughts: "What was this man flourishing the note for? Perhaps for change." (p. 163). By using this narrative technique the reader is asked to adopt the two different viewpoints and thus made to empathise with both characters. However, the presentation of the two men differs in the degree of irony employed by the narrator which becomes obvious when looking at how the American is referred to: The "red-faced man" is clearly the one to whom the narrator has adopted a greater distance (expressed in the irony used).

Background Information: Kalki Avatar

The tenth avatar, Kalki, is the final reincarnation of the Hindu god Vishnu who will end the Kali Yuga, the time of darkness and destruction. The horse is therefore a symbol for the Hindu belief in a redeemer coming to end the current time of destruction and darkness. Concerning the time, place and reasons for the appearance of the Kalki Avatar there are various assumptions. The rider on a white horse is a popular image of the Kalki Avatar symbolizing the messiah. In one of the Sanskrit languages Kalki Avatar means "White Horse".

Teaching Suggestions

Pre-Reading Activities

1. Miming

All the students are asked not to talk while carrying out this task.

Some students are given sentences to be communicated to the rest of the class without talking. The rest of the class tries to write down their guesses.

Use the following sentences:

– "I am hungry."
– "I would like to marry your daughter."
– "I am from New York."
– "I would like to buy your T-Shirt."

Then discuss the importance of gestures and facial expressions for communication.

2. On the bazaar

Imagine you are in a foreign country where none of the languages you are familiar with is understood. Set up a scene with your partner how you would try to inform a trader on the bazaar about something you would like to buy.

3. Meta-communication

How do you communicate your wishes and feelings?

How could you communicate them when others don't speak the same language as you?

While-Reading Activities

1. p. 158, ll. 15–18

The old man mistakes the American for a police officer. Explain what leads to this assumption. How does this account for his reaction?

2. p. 163, ll. 11–13

The American takes bank notes from his wallet. How do you expect the old man to react? What are the conclusions he might draw?

After-Reading Activity / Analysis

Analysis of main characters and their cultural backgrounds

Go through the text in your team and analyse the topics each of the men talk about with the help of the table given below.

What does this tell you about them as a character with a particular cultural background?

Old Man		American	
what we can find out about him	topic he talks about	topic he talks about	what we can find out about him
feels questioned and answers	"My name is Muni." → personal information	"How do you do?" → small talk	behaves in a typically American way of being polite

Division of the text into 5 sections

Team 1: p.158 l.4 "Marvellous!..." – l.27 "...anything may happen."

Team 2: p.158 l.28 "I am sure..." – p.160 l.14 "...don't remember him."

Team 3: p.160 l.15 "Because I really..." – p.162 l.14 "...to death..."

Team 4: p.162 l.16 "At this stage..." – p.164 l.6 "...the red-faced man said."

Team 5: p.164 l.7 "You'd better talk..." – p.166 l.7 "...down to wait"

Topics for Class Discussion

1. **What is the relevance of "souvenirs" like the horse in the story in our Western world? What does it mean to the American to own the horse?**

2. **"Inter-human communication procedures are either symmetric or complementary, depending on whether the relationship of the partners is based on differences or parity." (Paul Watzlawick)**

   – **Is communication symmetric or complementary in the story? Give reasons.**

   – **What is the basis of communication in the story?**

3. **The two men meeting for the first time are not familiar with the other's cultural background and life style.**

   – What do they do in order to overcome that discrepancy?

   – Do they succeed in applying their tactics?

4. **The old man has the money to open the shop, the American gets the statue of the horse.**

   – Does the story end in a win-win-constellation?

   – Who is the winner for you?

Creative Writing

1. **Turning the short story into a scene**
   Choose one section of the meeting between the two men that seems most striking for you.
   Go through the text and write down what is said in this section.
   Then decide on how you want to present this section to the rest of the class. You should also think about props and include stage directions with your dialogue and turn it into a scene to be acted out.

2. **Writing a travel diary or web log**
   Imagine the American businessman had his own web log and that every night he writes into his travel diary about the events of the day. Write such a web log entry for him and think of links or pictures he might wish to include.

3. **Personal motto**
   Imagine each of the two men had to be given a motto for their attitudes towards life. What could it be? Explain your choice.

4. **Finding an ending**
   After the old man has left the American sits down to wait. What do you think will happen? Write an ending concentrating on either what becomes of the old man or the American.

Composition

1. "This statue, like scores of similar ones scattered along the countryside, was forgotten and unnoticed, with lantana and cactus growing around it. Even the youthful vandals of the village left the statue alone, hardly aware of its existence."
   – What attitude of the villagers does the narrator seem to convey? Why?

2. The American is referred to as "the red-faced man" by the narrator throughout the story.
   – What does this indicate?

3. Will the American take the statue with him or not? Find evidence in the text.

4. The tenth avatar, Kalki, is the final reincarnation of the Hindu god Vishnu who will end the Kali Yuga, the time of darkness and destruction. The redeemer is often represented by a white horse. What could the white horse from the story be compared to in your own culture? What would be the value of such a statue for you?

Topics for Presentations

1. Give a brief view into the idea of cultural imperialism.
   http://www.wsu.edu:8001/vcwsu/commons/topics/culture/culture-index.html

2. Give a view into the reactions of the Indian public to Narayan's works. You may use the special Frontline edition by The Hindu.
   http://www.hinduonnet.com/fline/fl1811/index.htm

3. Inform your classmates about the beliefs and practices in Hinduism.
   http://www.bbc.co.uk/religion/religions/hinduism/index.shtml

Ngugi wa Thiong'o
"A Meeting in the Dark" (1975)

Interpretation and Background Information

Ngugi wa Thiong'o's "A Meeting in the Dark"

Ngugi's story "A Meeting in the Dark" is one of the later short stories from the collection *Secret Lives* published in 1975. The stories in this collection are organized loosely chronologically and give an insight into Kenyan history, beginning with the Gikuyu myths and moving on to the Emergency in the 1950s, and on to the post-Emergency, independence and post-independence periods. "A Meeting in the Dark" throws light and not a little darkness on the clash between native and Western culture, specifically here between Kenyans with traditional beliefs and those who have adopted the beliefs of Christian missionaries.

Description and Summary of "A Meeting in the Dark"

John, an adolescent Kenyan accepted at Makerere University in Uganda, has a problem, a rather universal one in fact, in both real life and narrative literature – he has impregnated the beautiful but uneducated Wamuhu. John's parents, unlike Wamuhu's, are Christians, having been christianized by missionaries at Fort Hall, especially John's father Stanley, who is now a Bible-thumping preacher. "He preached with great vigour, defying the very gates of hell. Even during the Emergency, he had gone on preaching, scolding, judging and condemning. All those who were not saved were destined for hell. Above all, Stanley was known for his great and strict moral observances – a bit too pharisaical in nature." (p. 186) His mother has acquiesced to the new religion, though her connection to the old ways are still present. "He even made her stop telling stories to the child. 'Tell him of Jesus. Jesus died for you. Jesus died for the child. He must know the Lord.' She, too, had been converted. But she was never blind to the moral torture he inflicted on the boy (that was how she always referred to John), so that the boy had grown up mortally afraid of his father." p. 171) John's difficulties are compounded by his not being able to tell his father what he has done. Caught between two worlds, John can't decide whether he should pursue his future at the university or marry Wamuhu (not that he really has a choice).

Ngugi concentrates on the conflict raging inside the boy and in his inability to make a decision. The tension increases as we watch John squirm, so to speak, on the horn of his dilemma. When his father asks him if he plans on taking a walk into the village, John says, "Well-yes-no. I mean, nowhere in particular." (p. 169) "He stood doubtfully in front of his father. His heart beat faster and there was that anxious voice within him asking: Does he know?" (p. 169) "John shrank within himself with fear." (p. 170) "A pain rose in his heart and he felt like crying [to his village] – I hate you, I hate you! You trapped me alive. Away from you it would have never happened." (p. 173) In the hut of Wamuhu's parents, "John bit his lip again and felt like bolting. He controlled himself with difficulty." (p. 177) He accuses of Wamuhu of tricking him into impregnating her, but "knew he was lying." (p. 180) "He felt desperate. Next week he would go to the college." (p. 180) "He could not possibly face his father. Or his mother. Or Reverend Carstone who had had such faith in him." (p. 181) "The night of reckoning had come. And he had not thought of anything." (p. 187)

"He simply could not make up his mind." (p. 188) "Whatever he did looked fatal to him." (p. 188) "John stands there trembling like the leaf of a tree on a windy day." (p. 190)

With admirable narrative pacing (for example, we don't learn that he has impregnated Wamuhu until the midpoint of the story ["Look, Wamuhu, how long have you been pre- . . . I mean, like this?" (p. 180)]), Ngugi takes us to the point where madness overtakes John and in a frenzy he murders the girl. The story's quite unsubtle final line is: "Soon everyone will know that he has created and then killed." (p. 190)

The plot can be broken down into the following sequence of scenes:

1. John with his father and mother in their hut is interrogated by his father, and the more Stanley asks him questions, the more guilty John feels. We learn in this opening that he is to take a journey next week, though we don't yet know that the journey refers to his entering the university in Uganda.

2. When John leaves the hut, Susana, John's mother, finally speaks and asks her husband why he persecutes the boy. Stanley reflects that "Really, women could never understand." (p. 172) This scene establishes the relationship between this couple and develops their characters. On the surface she is relegated to an inferior role, but we also learn that although he puts himself in a superior moral position by demanding that her soul be saved, he also fears his wife ("It was a surprise, but it seemed he feared his wife." [p. 172]) and evades an open confrontation with her: "He was startled by the vehemence in her voice. He had never seen her like this. Lord, take the devil out of her. Save her this minute. She did not say what she wanted to say. Stanley looked away from her. [. . .] He took his Bible and began to read." (p. 172) Though Stanley's perspective dominates in this scene, it opens and closes with Susana's.

3. John strolls through the village and he looks at it as if it were the source of his dilemma. "You trapped me alive!" (p. 173). He meets a village woman carrying home firewood and politely answers her question about his upcoming "journey" to Makerere University. "John was by nature polite [. . .] quite unlike the other proud, educated sons of the tribe-sons who came back from the other side of the waters with white or Negro wives who spoke English. [. . .] John would never betray the tribe." (p. 173–74) The woman "moved on, panting like a donkey, but she was obviously pleased with John's politeness." (p. 174)

4. Three brief transition scenes follow:
   a) John continues his stroll and meets in "the small local tea-shop" several villagers "who wished him well at the college. All of them knew that the priest's son had finished all the whiteman's learning in Kenya. He would now go to Uganda. They had read this in the *Baraza*, the Swahili Weekly." (p. 175)
   b) Back home for another brief scene: the evening meal set, John sees that "his father was still at the table reading his Bible. He did not look up when John entered. Strange silence settled in the hut." (p. 175) To his mother he lies about not being unhappy, then goes to his own hut. "Every young man had his own hut." (p. 175)
   c) John in his hut takes his coat and cap, leaves the "lantern burning, so that his father would see it and think he was in. John bit his lower lip spitefully. He hated himself for being so girlish. It was unnatural for a boy of his age." (p. 175–76)

5. Back to the village streets, where "young men and women [. . .] were laughing, talking, whispering [. . .] obviously enjoying themselves. John thought, they are more free than I am. [. . .] They clearly stood outside or above the strict morality that the educated ones had to be judged by." (p. 176) Then, "at the very heart of the village" he comes to the hut of Wamuhu and her parents. Inside, "[t]he flame and the giant shadow created on the wall seemed to be mocking him." (p. 176) The parents are proud that someone like John has come to visit. "To be visited by such an educated one, who knew all about the whiteman's world and knowledge and who would now go to another land beyond, was not such a frequent occurrence that it could be taken lightly." (p. 177) Too nervous to wait for Wamuhu's return, John bolts and outside "almost collided with Wamuhu." (p. 177)

6. Back in the hut for a scene with Wamuhu's parents. "A clergyman's son!" exclaims the father. "You forget your daughter is circumcised." (The fact that "circumcision" is a euphemism for female genital cutting is a detail the story elides.) The father reflects on the tribal ways (e.g. that his wife was a virgin when he married her) and compares them to *the whiteman's ways*. "Then the white men had come, preaching a strange religion, strange ways, which all men followed. The tribe's code of behaviour was broken. The new faith could not keep the tribe together. How could it? The men who followed the new faith would not let the girls be circumcised." (p. 178) He contradicts his wife when she tries to defend John. "Different! Puu! They are all alike. Those coated with the white clay of the whiteman's ways are the worst. They have nothing inside. Nothing – nothing here.' [. . .] He trembled. And he feared; he feared for the tribe." (p. 178–79) When the father asks his wife if she's noticed their daughter acting strangely, she does not respond, "preoccupied with her own great hopes." (p. 179)

7. John and Wamuhu walk through the village streets, with John pondering his options. "Why should he feel ashamed? The girl was beautiful, probably the most beautiful girl in the whole of Limuru. Yet he feared being seen with her. It was all wrong. He knew that he could have loved her; even then he wondered if he did not love her." (p. 179) In dialogue we learn that Wamuhu has granted him a week before she tells her parents that she's pregnant. "A week is over today," she says. (p. 179) "Darkness was now between them. He was not really seeing her; before him was the image of his father – haughtily religious and dominating. Again he thought: I, John, a priest's son, respected by all and going to college, will fall, fall to the ground. He did not want to contemplate the fall." (p. 180) At this point he blurts out that it was the girl's fault, though "he knew he was lying." The crisis of decision once more upon him and once again unable to decide ("He did not know what to do."), he recalls a story his mother once told him, one that foreshadows the fate of Wamuhu. "*Once upon a time there was a young girl . . . she had no home to go to and she could not go forward to the beautiful land and see all the good things because the Irimu [cannibal monster] was on the way . . .* " (p. 180) John feels "desperate" and "frightened", and with "a sad note of appeal" in his voice asks her how long she's been pregnant. (This is the first time we're given direct information about the cause of his dilemma.) For three months, she reminds him. John asks for three more weeks reprieve, at which she laughs. "Ah! The little witch!" John thinks. He tells her that he'll let her know tomorrow. She agrees. "Tomorrow. I cannot wait any more unless you mean to marry me." (p. 181)

8. Alone again, he collapses on the ground ("He could not move but sank on the ground in a heap. Sweat poured profusely down his cheeks, as if he had been running hard under a strong sun." [p. 181]) and ponders his situation. "He could not possibly face his father. Or his mother. Or Reverend Carstone who had had such faith in him. John realized that, though he was

educated, he was no more secure than anybody else. He was no better than Wamuhu. Then why don't you marry her? He did not know. John had grown up under a Calvinistic father and learnt under a Calvinistic headmaster – a missionary!" (p. 181–82) But the thought of praying to "Carstone's God" seems "false. It was as if he was blaspheming. Could he pray to the God of the tribe? His sense of guilt crushed him." (p. 182) He falls to sleep on the ground and when he awakes he feels better knowing he has one more day before he has to make his decision. As he walks home in the dark ("darkness blanketed the whole earth and him in it" [p. 182]), he hears the laughter and quarreling of families in their huts. "Little fires could be seen flickering red through the open doors. Village stars, John thought. He raised up his eyes. The heavenly stars, cold and distant, looked down on him impersonally." (p. 182) No clearer image can be found in the story of the sense of community and happiness that tribal life offers him. But acculturation has weakened John physically, psychologically, and morally. "John consoled himself by thinking that [the children at play] would come to face their day of trial." (p. 182) He continues to dither about whether or not he should marry Wamuhu and reflects on her lack of education. "If only Wamuhu had learning . . . and she was uncircumcised . . . then he might probably rebel." (p. 183) Thinking he isn't strong enough to face his parents, he returns to his own hut.

9. He awakes from a dream about initiation and circumcision, in which "ghosts from all sides [. . .] pulled him from all sides so that his body began to fall into pieces" until he becomes "nothing, nothing . . ." "Dreams about circumcision were no good. They portended death." (p. 184) But John shrugs off the dream "with a laugh" and opens the window onto a landscape that brings him as close to self-recognition as he will come.

> The hills, ridges, valleys and plains that surrounded the village were lost in the mist. It looked such a strange place. But there was almost a magic fascination in it. Limuru was a land of contrasts and evoked differing emotions at different times. Once John would be fascinated and would yearn to touch the land, embrace it or just be on the grass. At another time he would feel repelled by the dust, the strong sun and the pot-holed roads. If only his struggle were just against the dust, the mist, the sun and the rain, he might feel content. Content to live here. At least he thought he would never like to die and be buried anywhere else but at Limuru. But there was the human element whose vices and betrayal of other men were embodied in the new ugly villages. The last night's incident rushed into his mind like a flood, making him weak again. [. . .] An odd feeling was coming to him – in fact had been coming – that his relationship with his father was perhaps unnatural. But he dismissed the thought. [. . .] It was unfortunate that this scar had come into his life at this time, when he was going to Makerere and it would have brought him closer to his father. (p. 184–85)

As he shops that day with his father in the village at the businesses of "lanky but wistful Indian traders", he thinks about his father, about his moral rectitude, and about the church members who cannot follow his strict behaviour. But then Stanley himself had "fallen before his marriage" (he had sexual intercourse with Susana before they were married). Stanley "was also a product of the disintegration of the tribe due to the new influences." (p. 186–87) When they return home, his father asks him why he wasn't at prayers the night before, and John once again inwardly rebels: "Why do you ask me?" he thinks. "What right have you to know where I was? One day I am going to revolt against you. But immediately, John knew that this act of rebellion was something beyond him – unless something happened to push him into it." (p. 187) Rather than rebel, all he can do is stutter a response, as he did to a question of his father's at the story's beginning: "I – I – I mean, I was . . ." The father detects something odd in his son's voice, but "John went away relieved" (p. 187) that he's avoided again telling his father the truth.

10. In the final scene, still indecisive, John goes out again at night to meet Wamuhu. "John dressed like the night before and walked with faltering steps towards the fatal place. The night of reckoning had come. And he had not thought of anything." (p. 187) He recalls Reverend Carstone's last words to him. "You are going into the world. The world is waiting even like a hungry lion, to swallow you, to devour you. Therefore, beware of the world. Jesus said, Hold fast unto . . .' John felt a pain – a pain that wriggled through his flesh as he remembered these words. [. . .] Yes! He, John, would fall from the Gates of Heaven down through the open waiting Gates of Hell." (p.188) He arrives with nothing to tell the girl, still unable to decide. "He simply could not make up his mind." (p. 188) Then he tries to buy Wamuhu off, offering more and more money, insulting and saddening her. In his desperation, John goes mad, his mind splits between what he thinks he is doing and what he is doing in reality. The story's tense also breaks down, when it shifts for the first time from past to present. "The figure was rapidly rising – nine thousand, ten thousand, twenty thousand . . . He is mad. He is foaming. He is quickly moving towards the girl in the dark." One part of him calls "her by all sorts of endearing words" while the other part of grabs her by the neck and throttles her. "She lets out one horrible scream and then falls on the ground. And so all of a sudden, the struggle is over, the figures stop, and John stands there trembling like the leaf of a tree on a windy day" (p. 190), the simile showing him as weak and indecisive to the end.

Between Two Worlds

Like all adolescents, John is in a liminal zone, neither here nor there. For most of us, though a difficult place (and time) to be in, this threshold between youth and young adulthood is protean and generative. Possibilities abound and hope is the air we breathe. But John, about to leave Kenya and enter a university in Uganda, doesn't so much stand on the threshold as collapse in front of it.

A good boy, polite and educated at the missionary school, raised in a Christian home by a father who is a preacher, John, for all his acculturation, is also weak and worried and terrified of his father and life. Near the end, bluntly, objectively, the story states John's problem: "He simply could not make up his mind." (p. 188) Time and again the story shows him in a state of indecision. "Well-yes-no," he says to his father. Only by delaying his decision can he maintain his sanity. After being given a day's reprieve by Wamuhu, he falls to the ground and passes out. Then: "He woke up. Where was he? Then he understood. Wamuhu had left him. She had given him one day. He stood up; he felt good. Weakly, he began to walk back home." (p. 182) (The movement in physical space back and forth between his family's home and the village is an apt metaphor for his situation.)

Not that his dilemma is an easy one to solve – to marry the village girl he has impregnated and thus give up college or to . . . what? What's his real alternative to this scenario? He's not about to ask either his father or mother for help, terrified as he is of his father and too ashamed, perhaps, to tell his mother. Nor, it seems, is there anyone else he's close enough to to ask. No friends, no adults, no relatives for him to go to. What has caused this sad state of affairs? Is it his acculturation, that he's no longer truly native?

In many ways it seems that the choice John needs to make is more between two cultures than it is between Wamuhu or college. Should he decide in favor of his village or the great, white-inflected elsewhere? But his problem, as we've amply seen and been directly told, is that he cannot make a decision. Why can't he? Is his problem unsolvable? For him it is, because, the story suggests, he has been tainted by *the whiteman's ways*. "Those coated with the white clay of the whiteman's ways are the worst," says Wamuhu's father, whose sorrow for what he sees happening to his tribe is forcefully portrayed. "The old man trembled and cried inside[,] mourning for a tribe that had crumbled. The tribe had nowhere to go to. And it could not be what it was before." (p. 179)

Though John both loves and hates his country, with the exception of a few potholes in the streets, the village seems like a pretty attractive place. Children laugh and play, the people John meets are admiring of him and friendly, and Wamuhu is beautiful and true to her word not to tell anyone what has happened to her. (What *her* choices are isn't explored, but then she's not the protagonist, "only" the one he's impregnated.) Those who are not torn between native culture and missionary influences seem to lead a much happier life, as exemplified by the woman John meets on his way to the village: "What made such a woman live on day to day, working hard, yet happy? Had she much faith in life? Or was her faith in the tribe? She and her kind, who had never been touched by ways of the whiteman, looked as though they had something to cling to." (p. 174) Those living according to the Kenyan set of values seem to enjoy a more carefree and less troubled life than John. This contrast becomes obvious as John walks though the streets on his way to Wamuhu: "He met young men and women lining the streets. They were laughing, talking, whispering. They were obviously enjoying themselves. John thought, they are more free than I am. He envied their exuberance. They clearly stood outside or above the strict morality that the educated ones were judged by." (p. 176) Furthermore, the story's most lyrical passages of description occur when John looks closely at the village and the landscape. "He opened the window only to find the whole country clouded in mist. It was perfect July weather in Limuru. The hills, ridges, valleys and plains that surrounded the village were lost in the mist. It looked such a strange place. But there was almost a magic fascination in it." (p. 184)

So, again, why doesn't he simply say to hell with college, I'm staying here? Because the white-man's ways are in his mind now, they've altered his basic native character, or so the story seems to suggest. Christian guilt, the knowledge that he will fail and fall in the eyes of his father and his Father (though not Reverend Carstone's God, as is made clear), is as likely a suspect as any other. "He always looked at him as though John was a sinner, one who had to be watched all the time." (p. 169) His father has tried his best to deflect native influences, such as his wife's storytelling sessions with her son. He rejects the possibility of any rich blending between cultures, having "stopped his mother from telling him stories when he became a man of God. His mother had stopped telling him stories long ago. She would say to him, Now, don't ask for any more stories. Your father may come." (p. 169)

To Wamuhu's father it is clear that tribal culture and Christianity do not go together, but bring confusion to the people and make the tribe fall apart. Because of the white man's influence Kenyans no longer stick to the strict moral rules of no sex before marriage and are no longer circumcised.

> The tribe's code of behaviour was broken. The new faith could not keep the tribe together. How could it? The men who followed the new faith would not let the girls be circumcised. And they would not let their sons marry circumcised girls. Puu! Look at

what was happening. Their young men went away to the land of the white men. What did they bring? White women. Black women who spoke English. Aaa – bad. And the young men who were left just didn't mind. They made unmarried girls their wives and then left them with fatherless children. (p. 178)

When John disregards the warning his dream of being pulled apart by ghosts sends him and dismisses the dream "with a laugh", he deliberately cuts himself off from all tribal roots and knowledge and heads straight towards the fall he fears. In this young man, acculturation has produced an indecisive weakling. The dream was right. Rather than create a stronger identity, the pull of the two cultures causes his self to split ("'It was your fault.' [. . .] In his heart he knew was lying." [p. 180]), and then destroys it ("He is mad. He is foaming. [p. 189]). And the end result the story's last line hammers home: "Soon everyone will know that he has created and then killed." (p. 190)

Point of View

"A Meeting in the Dark" offers, among other things, a lesson in the flexibility, breadth, and focus of the *third person omniscient* point of view. With its omniscient narrator concealed (unlike in, say, Homer's *The Odyssey* where the omniscient narrator can speak directly to the reader in first person), third person omniscient, or *straight third person*, is capable of moving in and out of the consciousness of different characters and yet still maintain overall the objectivity of third person narration with its privilege of moving about in time and space. In "A Meeting in the Dark" the *point of view* is adaptable enough to enter the thoughts of four different characters: John, his father Stanley, his mother Susana, and Wamuhu's father. At one point it even shifts narrative modes by using the camera-like, *fly-on-the-wall technique* or *scenic method*. There is, then, no single character through whose eyes (body, mind, emotions) we experience the story, as one finds in *third-person limited omniscience*. Also known as *method of central intelligence*, third-person limited may enter the mind of one character only; other characters are perceived either from the objective third-person or through the eyes of the central intelligence.

Though we do not have one character through whom the universe of the story is filtered, John's point of view is the one that receives the most "air-time". He is after all, the story's protagonist, the one upon whom the story's motivation rests. And it's through his eyes the story opens: "He stood at the door of the hut and saw his old, frail but energetic father coming along the village street, with a rather dirty bag made of a strong calico swinging by his side. His father always carried this bag. John knew what it contained . . ." (p. 169) The ready avenue into the thoughts of a character offered by the straight third-person point of view can be seen in such passages as the following: "John shrank within himself with fear. [. . .] He felt no doubt his father knew all about it. He thought: 'Why does he torture me? Why does he not at once say he knows?' Then another voice told him: 'No, he doesn't know, otherwise he would have already jumped at you.'" (p. 170) Once the possibility of interiority is established, the author need not indicate the shift with "She thought" or "She felt". The following is a complete paragraph from the story: "Why not marry her? She is beautiful! Why not marry? Do I love her or don't I?" (p. 181) However, to maintain its objectivity, the omniscient narrator doesn't remain long within John's mind: "Why do you ask me? What right have you to know where I was? One day I am going to revolt against you. But, immediately, John knew that this act of rebellion was something beyond him" (p. 187). (Note: In this story, we never stay long enough within the mind of any one character or go deep enough into the mind to have examples of either *interior monologue* or *stream of consciousness*.)

To a lesser degree than John's point of view, the narrative perspective shifts to John's father Stanley ("Really, women could never understand. Women were women, whether saved or not. Their son had to be protected against all evil influences. He must be made to grow in the footsteps of the Lord. He looked at her, frowning a little. She had made him sin but that had been a long time ago. And he had been saved. John must not tread the same road." [p. 171–72]); his mother's, though only in one scene ("Or could it be a resentment because, well, they two had 'sinned' before marriage? John had been the result of that sin. But that had not been John's fault. It was the boy who ought to complain. She often wondered if the boy had . . . but no. The boy had been very small when they left Fort Hall." [p. 171]; "She did not know what was troubling her son. Was it the coming journey? Still, she feared for him." [p. 172]), and Wamuhu's father's ("The old man was remembering his own day. He had found for himself a good virtuous woman, initiated in all the tribe's ways. And she had known no other man." [p. 178]; "A strange numbness came over him. He trembled. And he feared; he feared for the tribe. For now he saw it was not only the educated men who were coated with strange ways, but the whole tribe. The old man trembled and cried inside mourning for a tribe that had crumbled." [p. 178–79]).

Still, we shouldn't overemphasize these instances of interiority, for objective third-person narrative description dominates the narrative perspective. There's even a moment, in the directness of its judgment, when the omniscient narrator almost speaks to us in first person: "The trouble with John was that his imagination magnified the fall from the heights of 'goodness' out of all proportion. And fear of people and consequences ranked high in the things that made him contemplate the fall with so much horror." (p. 188) Another instance of narrative objectivity that calls attention to itself is when John leaves the hut of Wamuhu's parents and bumps into her outside and the story abruptly moves from the exterior "shot" to an interior one by stating: "In the hut: 'Didn't I tell you? Trust a woman's eye!'" (p. 177), as if we were reading a play or film script.

A radical shift, closely linked to point of view, comes at the end of the story when, within a paragraph, we shift from past to present tense. In this instance, it's John's state of mind (overwhelmed, frenetic, psychotic) that triggers the sprung tense.

> The figure was rapidly rising – nine thousand, ten thousand, twenty thousand . . . He is mad. He is foaming. He is quickly moving towards the girl in the dark. He has lain his hands on her shoulders and is madly imploring her in a hoarse voice. Deep inside him, something horrid that assumes the threatening anger of his father and the village seems to be pushing him. He is violently shaking Wamuhu, while his mind tells him that he is patting her gently. (p. 189)

Finally, what exactly is the point of view of the story's last line? "Soon everyone will know that he has created and then killed." If John's, then it puts in question how mad he is really is at the time he murders the girl; he seems more concerned with what others think of him than with what he's done. If it's an authorial "objective" perspective, it reveals a tendency to elevate idea over character. Unlike John who cannot process cultural contradictions, perhaps we should grant the last line a double perspective.

Background Information: Female Genital Mutilation

Tucked inside two passages of interior thought is an obviously important yet unexplored opposition in the story between native Kenyan and Western thought. In fact, if we don't look closely it goes unnoticed, since it's mentioned only in passing. Wamuhu's father bemoans a world where girls are not "circumcised", whereas John thinks that if Wamuhu were more educated and "uncircumcised", he might be able to rebel against his father.

> The tribe's code of behaviour was broken. The new faith could not keep the tribe together. How could it? The men who followed the new faith would not let the girls be circumcised. And they would not let their sons marry circumcised girls. Puu! (p. 178)

> Women's education was very low. Perhaps that was why so many Africans went "away" and came back married. He too wished he had gone with the others, especially in the last giant student airlift to America. If only Wamuhu had learning . . . and she was uncircumcised . . .then he might probably rebel. (p. 183)

According to information available on the web sites of the WHO (World Health Organization) and Amnesty International, 85% of so-called "female circumcisions", i.e. female genital mutilations (FGMs) that are conducted in Africa consist of clitoridectomy and the excision of the labia minora. (For males, of course, no sexual organ is excised during circumcision.) 15% of these ritualistic mutilations in Africa are thought to be infibulations, a procedure which entails a clitoridectomy, the excision of the labia majora, and the stitching of the labia majora to cover the vagina. A small hole is left for purposes of urination and menstruation. The procedure is performed usually on girls between the ages of four and eight, sometimes in a group ritual, sometimes in a home, sometimes with medical supervision, more frequently not. An estimated 6000 mutilations occur every day in the world. The physical and psychological harm caused by FGM are, of course, severe and under-documented. The physical effects include urine retention, chronic infections, dermoid cysts, reproductive tract infections due to obstructed menstrual flow, kidney damage, severe haemorrhaging, and death. Of course, not to undergo the procedure sometimes also leads to death, often at the hands of a male family member.

The rationales given for this practice usually involve tradition and cultural identity. Amnesty International's article on FGM states that "[m]any people in FGM-practising societies, especially traditional rural communities, regard FGM as so normal that they cannot imagine a woman who has not undergone mutilation." Nor is it surprising, considering the patriarchal nature of societies that practice FGM, that cutting out the clitoris is seen as feminizing the girl, making her more docile and at the same time reducing her sexual desire, and thus more likely to be faithful to her future husband. As one Kenyan woman says, quoted in the Amnesty International article, "Circumcision makes women clean, promotes virginity and chastity and guards young girls from sexual frustration by deadening their sexual appetite."

Alas, having her genitals cut out did not stop unmarried Wamuhu from having sex with John.

For more information, go to: www.who.int/topics/female_genital_mutilation/en/ www.amnesty.org/ailib/intcam/femgen/fgm1.html

Implications and Assessment

If fiction is a mirror put up to reality, then there's a distortion in the glass of "A Meeting in the Dark", for the story seems to romanticize tradition: the mother as the vessel of tradition and truth in her role as culture's story teller; the beautiful girl who is killed; the happy villagers; John's prophetic dream; etc. Identity seen as something static rather than fluid is part of what makes the story problematic. History, surely, offers ample reasons to suspect any call for racial or cultural purity. (For Ngugi's take on related matters see the two excerpts from essays by the author in this volume [p. 311–315].)

But considered in terms of character, the story is an accurate portrayal of an adolescent caught between two cultures, beset by conflicting desires and demands, made weak in spirit by being neither native nor Christian, and unmanned ("He hated himself for being so girlish. It was unnatural for a boy of his age." [p. 176]). What saves Ngugi's story from one-dimensionality is the existential, trans-cultural dilemma the boy suffers and the author's ability to make the reader experience it. At times the narrative achieves an almost Dostoyevskian intensity.

Perhaps, though, what's finally most terrifying about "A Meeting in the Dark" isn't what it tells us about two cultures in conflict but what it doesn't say about female oppression. After all, it's not only her clitoris Wamuhu has had removed, but also her life.

Teaching Suggestions

Pre-Reading Activities

1. On the basis of the story's title, have the students guess the story's content. What associations can they come up with the nouns "meeting" and "dark"?

2. Have the students cite instances they know of where cultural divisions within a country have led to great harm.

While-Reading Activity

As they move through the story, have the students follow the trail of John's indecisiveness and note down those moments where key information is delivered (e.g., the points where they learn John's "journey" is about his leaving for college in Uganda and they learn that Wamuhu is pregnant).

After-Reading Activities / Analysis

1. Why does Ngugi shift to present tense at the end? What are the effects of this shift? What does it tell you about the state of John's mind?

2. How is the village described? What implications can you draw from these descriptions? Does the author take a stand for or against village life?

Topics for Class Discussion

1. What are the advantages of the author's choice of third person omniscient point of view? (See "Point of View" above.)

2. Draw the students' attention to the ethical dimension of the story by offering the follow topic for discussion: John – coward and murderer or victim of circumstance?

3. John is caught between cultures. Discuss in what ways the Christian and native cultures are in conflict with one another. How else is John "caught in the middle"? (See "Between Two Worlds" above.)

4. Discuss the issue of female "circumcision" (i.e. female genital cutting). Where is it mentioned in the story? What does the story tell and not tell us about this practice? (See "Background Information: Female Genital Mutilation" above.)

Creative Writing

Although at times we have access to John's thoughts, we never enter fully enough to call these passages either stream of consciousness or interior monologue. Now's your chance. Write down his thoughts and feelings directly after the murder. Remember that he may not be in his right mind. (Before the students begin to write, you may want to give them examples of interior monologues from Faulkner's *As I Lay Dying* or Molly Bloom's interior monologue in the last section of Joyce's *Ulysses*.)

Topics for Presentations

1. **Give a report on the life and career of Ngugi wa Thiong'o.**
   www.kirjasto.sci.fi/ngugiw.htm
   www.scholars.nus.edu.sg/post/poldiscourse/ngugiov.html
   en.wikipedia.org/wiki/Ngugi_wa_Thingo
   Updike, John: *Hugging the Shore*. Knopf, 1983. p. 697–701. (Review of Ngugi's novel *Petals of Blood*)

2. **Prepare a presentation on Kenya. Include geographical as well as political information. Also give a short overview of Kenyan history.**
   en.wikipedia.org/wiki/Kenya
   www.cia.gov/cia/publications/factbook/geos/ke.html
   www.kenyaweb.com

3. **Give a presentation on the ritualistic practice of female genital mutilation.**
   www.who.int/topics/female_genital_mutilation/en/
   www.amnesty.org/ailib/intcam/femgen/fgm1.html
   Dirie,Waris: *Desert Flower*. Virago Press, 2001.

Muriel Spark
"The Black Madonna" (1958)

Interpretation and Background Information

Muriel Spark's "The Black Madonna"

"The Black Madonna" was first published in 1958 in a collection of short stories entitled *The Go-Away Bird and Other Stories* (London: Macmillan), at a time at which serious efforts to respect and appreciate the culture of immigrants to the UK had not yet been made.

Short Interpretation of "The Black Madonna"

The opening paragraphs of the short story describe the black Madonna as if she was one of the main characters. It is only after this lengthy depiction of this bog-oak statue as well as a rather detailed description of the imaginary city of Whitney Clay that the two principal characters – Raymond and Lou Parker, a middle-aged couple, who have been married for 15 years – appear. An omniscient narrator then informs us at length about this childless couple, their habits and their daily life. Thus the story's exposition is rather traditional. The reader slowly glides into the action after having gained a general impression of the story's setting, central object and principal characters.

Soon after the couple's habits have been described, two new characters – Henry Pierce and Oxford St. John, Raymond`s Jamaican colleagues at the motors works – show up and trigger off the plot. The childless couple become more and more attached to these two black colleagues and end up spending a major portion of their time with them, showing them off to all of their friends although, as their novelty wears off, the couple's relationship to them becomes more and more distanced. Lou especially is glad that Henry is sent off to a sanatorium in Wales and will soon leave the country and that Oxford is going to Manchester.

Only one thing is missing in the couple's life – children. Finally Lou hears about the black Madonna's miraculous powers and, by praying to her, the couple finally manage to have a child of their own. Soon after the birth of their daughter, however, it becomes clear the child will be black. The genetic explanation for this, proven later by blood tests, is that an ancestor of Lou's was black, but the neighbours of course attribute the child's colour to Henry's and Oxford's regular appearance at the Parkers' apartment, thus putting the couple's alleged liberalism and openness towards blacks to the test. Not willing to raise a black child, which, although it is their own, everybody else thinks is not, Lou decides to put the child up for adoption.

In "The Black Madonna" Muriel Spark relies on a shock technique, which a number of her novels, among others *The Girls of Slender Means* and *The Prime of Miss Jean Brodie*, make use of as well. It consists of opposing appearance and reality and incites the reader to look at the ugly truth hidden behind a shiny surface. The Parkers' liberal pretensions concerning blacks collide shockingly with their racism, which is only revealed towards the end of the story when neither of them is able to accept the coloured baby even though it is their own.

Although Spark converted to Catholicism and her conversion more or less coincided with her success as a novelist, she nevertheless throws a rather critical and ironical light on the Catholic Church in "The Black Madonna" by revealing the hypocrisy of some of its members.

Narrator/Point of View

Told by an omniscient narrator, who comments ironically, if not cynically, on the story's plot from time to time, we see the story from a detached point of view, allowing us to see the characters' flaws and hidden feelings. It is typical of Spark to use the omniscient authorial voice in a whimsical, unexpected way, jerking the reader about on the end of a string.

Often the reader has to infer what the characters are really like from Spark's indirect hinting at things: *"All along he had known she was not a snob, only sensible, but he had rather feared she would consider the mixing of their new black and their old white friends not sensible."* (p. 199) This is a very indirect way of describing Lou's racial prejudices, which later drive her to give away her own child. The same goes for the following sentence: *"He kept referring to himself as black, which of course he was, Lou thought, but it was not the thing to say."* (p. 208) (Spark applies the same method of indirection when she describes Lou's husband.: *"Their visitors now were ordinary white ones. 'Not so colourful;' Raymond said ...* (p. 212)

Background Information: Black Madonnas

Black Madonnas, most of which are sculpted out of wood, can be found throughout the world. There are examples of black Madonnas in Belgium, Croatia, Ecuador, England, France, Germany, Hungary, Ireland, Italy, Lithuania, Luxembourg, Malta, Mexico, Poland, Romania, Sicily, Spain, Switzerland and the United States. However, there is not a single Madonna in the United Kingdom.

The theories of the origin of the Black Virgins vary, with Orthodox Catholics and reconstructive feminists having almost opposing views. Some Catholics say that the dark colour was used to match the skin pigmentation of the local population, others attribute the dark colour of the black Madonnas existing within light-skinned populations to a fire and subsequent soot or the accumulation of grime over the ages, or smoke from centuries of votive candles and, last but not least, the deterioration of lead-based pigments. Some Orthodox Catholics even go so far as to claim that artists deliberately created black Madonnas to illustrate the text from the Song of Songs, which reads: "I am black, but beautiful".

Many of the existing black Madonnas are found in France and date back to the time around the Crusades. The Templars and Cathars are said to have brought with them many black Madonnas on their return from the Crusades. Cathar symbolism represents figures with disproportionately large hands. The Templars followed the symbolism of the Eastern Orthodox Church, which describes the Madonna as the "Mother of the Light", who must have dark skin, because anything placed so close to the sun (Christ was symbolized as the light and the sun) must turn dark.

Others attribute the existence of black Madonnas to inculturation. In the course of its history the Catholic Church has incorporated the local indigenous pagan beliefs into their own church practices to aid in the assimilation of the newly converted to Catholicism. Thus some scholars claim that the black Madonna is the ancient earth-goddess (representing the fertility associated with black soil) converted to Christianity.

Some feminists believe the black Madonnas are the direct result of early matriarchal Africans travelling throughout the ancient world. Others claim that the influence of the Gypsies, who venerate the black goddess Sara, must not be underestimated.

Some suggest that the black colour of the Madonnas represents something archetypal and unexpressed in Christianity. Black represents the Death Mother, the Crone, the Shadow Self. In Catholic countries black is associated with magic and, not surprisingly, black Madonnas are often said to be much more powerful in performing miracles than their white counterparts.

The Black Madonna in Spark's Story

The black Madonna in Spark's story lends itself to a number of these interpretations. Of course the reference to the ancient earth-goddess representing fertility is more than obvious, but perhaps it is no coincidence that the miraculous powers of the black Madonna, said by some Catholics to owe their existence to the biblical line: "I am black, but beautiful" provide the desperate, childless couple with a black baby The black Madonna in the story is very powerful in performing miracles, as black Madonnas are said to be, even though Lou and Raymond Parker are confronted with a miracle that turns out quite different from what they anticipated, thus ultimately revealing their shadow self or their dark side, another feature connected with the black Madonna.

Teaching Suggestions

Pre-Reading Activities

The teacher shows the students a picture of a black Madonna. Since the Black Madonna mentioned in the story does not exist, a picture of a rather prominent black Madonna from Auvergne, France, has been printed on the transparency.

1. **Describe the picture.**
   - Have you ever seen anything like that?
   - What do you associate with a black Madonna?
   - Black Madonnas are said to grant a wish to those who pray to them. Imagine you are kneeling in front of a black Madonna. What would you wish for?
   What do you think a couple in their mid-thirties might wish for?

2. **read p.193, ll. 1–9**
   Compare the Black Madonna described in the story to the one on the transparency.

3. **Give the students the setting and the outline of the story and make them write a story of their own:**
   - black Madonna
   - Lou Parker (37), Raymond Parker, both Catholics, married for 15 years, middle-class
   - Henry Pierce, a Jamaican (24)
   - Oxford St. John, a Jamaican
   - Elizabeth, Lou's widowed sister, mother of eight children, very poor, living in Bethnel Green, a poor area of London

4. **Then compare the stories the students have written to Muriel Spark's "The Black Madonna".**

While-Reading Activities

1. **p. 193, l. 10 – p. 194, l. 3**
   Try to draw the town.

2. **p.193, l. 4 – p. 195, l. 7**
   Imagine Raymond and Lou Parker visit the church of the Black Madonna one day. What might they pray for as they stand in front of the black Madonna?

After-Reading Activity / Analysis

How can one explain Lou's complete rejection of the child in the end? Search for hidden traces of racism throughout the story.

Lou's complete rejection of Dawn Mary in the end can be explained by a sort of clandestine racism hitherto hidden beneath her Catholic charity and benevolence. Although she counts Henry Pierce and Oxford St. John among her friends and is proud to show them off, feeling a little special because she is one of the few to count two Jamaicans among her friends, there are slightly racist undertones, sometimes ironically commented on by the omniscient narrator, from the first time Henry Pierce and Oxford St. John are mentioned

Shortly after they have been introduced, Spark mentions that Henry and Oxford are black: *"They were unmarried, very polite and black"* (p.199), a feature which clearly seems to set them apart from the others. The fact that the colour of their skin is mentioned also means that having coloured friends is the exception rather than the rule in the society Raymond and Lou live in. All the more amazing is the fact that Lou Parker insists that every single one of their friends meet the two (cf. p. 199). Even her husband is bewildered by her behaviour and admits that *"he had rather feared she would consider the mixing of their new black and their old white friends not sensible"*, (cf. p. 199), seeming to be well aware of the fact that they thereby question, if not break, the widely accepted social conventions of Whitney Clay, or, more generally, of British society in the fifties.

Although Lou says that the two Jamaicans are "no different from anyone else" (p. 200) and urges her friend Tina Farrell not to refer to them as "darkies" (*"Well, don't call them darkies"*, p. 200), colour lines nevertheless turn out to be very strong, stronger than class lines even, as can be seen when the couple visits Lou's sister in Bethnel Green together with Henry. On this occasion Lou is very upset that Henry compares her sister to Jamaican women, for in her opinion *"at least Elizabeth's white!"* (p. 207). Shortly after, Henry Pierce withdraws from the couple's life, suddenly suffering from tuberculosis and has to be cured in a sanatorium in Wales.

Lou and Raymond now try to turn their affection to Oxford St. John, the other Jamaican colleague of Raymond's, who, however, being older and less docile, never quite manages to fill the vacancy Henry has left. With Oxford the racist undertones in Lou become obvious sooner than with Henry because he keeps referring to himself as *"black all over"* and, standing in front of the mirror, calls himself *"a big, black bugger"* (p. 208). He is aware of his blackness and takes pride in the colour of his skin when quoting the Song of Solomon from the *Old Testament* *"I am black but comely / O ye, daughters of Jerusalem"* (p. 208), which clearly shocks Lou. Although she does not comment verbally on this, her irritation is apparent to any sensitive reader: She drops stitches in her knitting and looks at the clock, hoping Oxford will soon be leaving. No longer able to incorporate this second Jamaican into her life, she feels nothing but relief to see Oxford leave for Manchester within three weeks.

Believing she has banned the colour issue from her life for good, the Empire ironically strikes back when her innermost wish of having a baby is finally granted by the bog-oak statue. Although the priest admonishes her to care for her infant (cf. p. 218), she puts the child up for adoption, saying: *"The baby's black and your blood tests can't make it white."* (p. 218)

1. **Do you think Lou will start sending money to her sister again once she has given her baby daughter up for adoption and no longer needs the money herself?**
   ad. lib.

2. **"It's just the thought of it being mine, and people thinking it isn't."**
   – Is that really the problem? Do Raymond and Lou just bow to the pressure of society? Or should they be held responsible for their own actions?
   ad. lib.

3. **Using your dictionary, find a definition of hypocrisy**
   – Are Lou and Raymond hyocrites?
   Hypocisy denotes a behaviour in which somebody pretends to have certain moral standards which they do not actually have. Raymond and Lou pretend to be good Catholics who are tolerant towards people from other countries, but then put up their own child for adoption because it has the wrong skin colour. They are hypocrites not only towards others but also towards themselves, not even aware of their own hypocrisy.

4. **Henry Pierce and Oxford St. John – a substitute for children?**
   Especially Henry Pierce seems to serve as a substitute son to the childless couple, bringing out *"the maternal in Lou, and to some extent the avuncular in Raymond"* (p. 201) Lou makes him read aloud her favourite poems and teaches him how to pronounce the words "jest" and "jollity" properly – like a mother teaching her child. When they go to London for a holiday, they take him with them, like parents spending their vacation with their son. (cf. p. 202)

Composition

What do you think – are class lines or racial lines stronger in Spark's story?
At the beginning of the story colour lines seem to be stronger than class lines. This becomes obvious when Raymond and Lou visit Lou's sister Elizabeth in Bethnel Green together with Henry. From the start Lou and Raymond are embarrassed to show Henry the dirty, smelly, run-down ground-floor flat Lou's sister Elizabeth lives in. After their visit to Lou's sister, Henry says: *"That sort (…) never moves. It's the slum mentality, man. Take some folks I've seen back home"* (p. 207), thereby comparing Elizabeth to women from Jamaica. Lou is outraged at his remark and immediately draws a clear line between her sister, who is white but underclass, and Henry, who has got a decent job at the motor works, but is black, by saying: *"There's no comparison (…) this is quite a different case"* (p. 201).
As soon as Lou knows she is pregnant, she stops supporting her sister, justifying her action by saying that they now need every penny themselves, thus not only withdrawing from their coloured friends Henry and Oxford, but also from her sister, rejecting everything that – either in color or in class – is different from her own environment.

Although Lou does not like to mention her Liverpudlian working class background, she is forced to confront both issues – class and colour – again when her baby Dawn Mary is born and finally resorts to putting the child up for adoption, an escape from, but not a solution to her problems, but one which allows her to keep up appearances and to continue to define herself as white and middle-class and clearly distinguish herself from the underclass or colored people.

Racism? Where does it start – where does it end? Can Raymond and Lou be called racist?
ad. lib.

Topics for Presentations

1. **Give a short talk on Jamaica and its relations to Great Britain. Include information on Jamaica's history and immigration from Jamaica to the UK.**

2. **Give a presentation on Mendel's law of heredity and explain to your classmates how it is possible for white parents (whose grandparents and even great-grandparents are all white) to have a black baby.**
The following Web site might prove helpful:
http://www.mendel-museum.org/eng/1online

3. ***"That sort (...) never moves. It's the slum mentality, man."* (p. 201) That is how Henry Pierce clearly classifies Lou's sister, Elizabeth, as belonging to the underclass.**
Give a short talk on the importance of class in British society. Put special emphasis on the British underclass.
The following Web sites might prove useful:
http:// elt.britcoun.org.pl/v_brclass.htm
http://www.academicdb.com/poverty_definition_cause_the possible_solutions_is_47

4. **Catholicism in the UK.**

Copymaster

Creative Writing

1 Imagine Lou Parker at age 60 surrounded by her London friends, many of whom have already become grandparents. One of her friends asks: "By the way, why have you and Raymond never had any children? Isn't it sad not to have any grandchildren?" How does Lou react? Write a possible answer to such a question.
ad. lib.

_____

_____

_____

2. The story begins with a detailed depiction of the Black Madonna (which almost gives her the status of a character), but surprisingly enough, she doesn't reappear in the end. Write a concluding paragraph to the short story in which she reappears. You may decide to include a personified version of the Black Madonna in which she speaks about what has happened.
ad. lib.

_____

_____

_____

_____

3. A mysterious object — the box of contraceptives
Raymond sees what he mistakenly takes for a box of contraceptives on Elizabeth's bedside table and later tells his wife about it, who is very upset about this. What do you think Elizabeth has on her bedside table and why?
ad. lib.

_____

_____

_____

_____

Salman Rushdie
"Good Advice is Rarer Than Rubies" (1987)

Interpretation and Background Information

Salman Rushdie's "Good Advice is Rarer Than Rubies"

In this story of ironic reversals, a young woman, offered the chance to relocate to England, refuses, preferring to remain in her own country of Pakistan. The colonialist assumption that West always bests East, is turned on its head.

Short Summary and Interpretation of "Good Advice is Rarer Than Rubies"

At dawn of an unspecified date (we only know that it's "the last Tuesday of the month" and in the second half of the 20th century), in an unspecified Pakistani town, a bus arrives out of which steps the beautiful Miss Rehana into "a cloud of dust" in front of the gates of the British Consulate. She contemplates the driver on the "beautiful bus" and the driver bows "theatrically as she descended" (p. 225).

The second paragraph introduces the story's central intelligence, the advice expert Muhammad Ali, an old man who scams women who come to the Consulate by giving them fraudulent advice on how to obtain their permits to travel to England. Except this time, because of Miss Rehana's beauty, the advice expert is not as rude as he usually is to his marks. Nor will she become one of his victims. The other women "all looked frightened", but not Miss Rehana who "did not seem at all alarmed", and Ali "found his feet leading him towards the strange, big-eyed, independent girl" (p. 226).

When he offers her advice for a fee, she says, "Good advice is rarer than rubies", but that she cannot pay him. "*I am going crazy*, Muhammad Ali thought", because he senses that Fate is telling him to give her advice, and *real* advice this time, for free. "Our meeting was written," he tells her. "I also am a poor man only, but for you advice comes free." Miss Rehana smiles at this. "Then I must surely listen" (p. 227).

He takes her to "his own special corner of the shanty-town" and while she eats chilli-pakoras and "two or three dozen pairs of male eyes" ogle her, "the old grey-haired fraud" begins to question her. When she hands over her application and asks him if it's correct, he detects "a note of anxiety in her voice" (p. 228). As he continues to tell her about what she is about to face when she confronts the British bureaucrats, the sahibs ("you are entering a worse place than any police station" (p. 229)), "Her innocence made him shiver with fear for her." Then he proceeds to explain to her the kinds of personal, intrusive questions she'll be asked. "Muhammad Ali spoke brutally, on purpose, to lessen the shock she would feel when it, or something like it, actually happened." If she makes one mistake, he tells her, "you are finished" (p. 230).

Again Ali reflects to himself that he normally doesn't do well by the women he gulls. "Life is hard, and an old man must live by his wits. It was not up to Muhammad Ali to have compassion for these Tuesday women." But instead of conning her, "his voice betrayed him" and he "began to reveal to her his greatest secret" (p. 231) – he offers her a British passport. "Anything was possible now, on this day of his insanity," he thinks. *The oldest fools are bewitched by the youngest girls*" (p. 232).

Unwilling to "commit a crime" (p. 232), Miss Rehana refuses, though he tells her it isn't a crime, calling it instead "Facilitation." But for her, to enter England illegally, "is not good advice." Having offered her more than he has anyone else, the advice expert is angered by her refusal, and shouts at her, "It is the curse of our people [...]. We are poor, we are ignorant, and we completely refuse to learn" (p. 233). The rest of the day he "did nothing but stand around near the Consulate gates" admonishing himself, until she comes back out and approaches him, appearing "calm, and at peace with him again, and he thought, *My god, ya Allah, she has pulled it off. The British sahibs also have been drowning in her eyes and she has got her passage to England*" (p. 234). She buys him pakoras for the two of them, and they sit on the bus's bumper, while he "began softly to hum a tune from a movie soundtrack" (p. 235), and she tells what happened and why.

"'It was an arranged engagement,' Miss Rehana said all at once. 'I was nine years old when my parents fixed it.'" Mustafa Dar is twenty-one years older than she. After her parents died, he went to England and promised to send for her. "That was many years ago. I have his photo, but he is like a stranger to me". Ali ponders this and comments that, though it is an arranged marriage, her parents were trying to look after her, and now she has "a lifetime to get to know [her husband], and to love" (p. 235).

Ah, but the advice expert has it all wrong, and Rushdie delivers the story's final reversal: Miss Rehana did not get her permit; she's happy because she has succeeded in failing. She intentionally gave the wrong answers to the questions the officials asked. "I completely redecorated, all absolutely topsy-turvy, you see" (p. 236). She has a job as a governess taking care of "three good boys" and has no intention of giving it up.

"But this is tragedy!" (p. 236) Ali moans, but Miss Rehana says he should not be sad.

"Her last smile, which he watched from the compound until the bus concealed it in a dust-cloud, was the happiest thing he had ever seen in his long, hot, hard, unloving life" (p. 237).

Rushdie's story has something of the quality of a fable about it. At times it seems more like an anecdote, a tale with a lesson in its tail. There's even a touch of magic to it, as if Fate had brought to the old advice expert a woman whose beauty is supernatural, capable of changing his "unloving life" and making him do something good. There is also a suggestion of the fantastic in her entering in a cloud of dust and departing in the same.

A gentle self-reflexivity is also at play in the story. The theatrical bow of the driver ushers in the heroine, who is about to take a rather surprising and edifyingly independent action. "Our meeting was written" (p. 227), Ali tells her, in a subtle self-reflexive gesture by Rushdie, whose post-modernist tendencies aren't usually so restrained.

Realistic details give balance and verisimilitude to the story – the pakoras, the dust, the coolies "tying their bedding rolls to the roof" (p. 235) of the bus, hawkers that shout at the people coming to the Consulate, the men in the shanty-town ogling Miss Rehana, the signs on the front and back of the bus.

"When Fate sends a gift," Miss Rehana says, "one receives good fortune" (p. 227). Ali (and the reader, since the story's point of view is limited to the old man's perspective) may believe Miss Rehana is being naive when she says this, but in fact, as it turns out, the reverse is true: what she says, we learn, is the case; good fortune does come her way.

Narrative Structure: Reversal and Recognition

Plot reversals, as Aristotle pointed out, are intimately linked to recognition, the change from ignorance to knowledge. In "Good Advice is Rarer Than Rubies" we expect the recognition to come to Miss Rehana. But she isn't in need of it. It's the old advice expert Muhammad Ali, from whose perspective the story is told, who does. The colonialist's assumption that the West will always be preferred to the East is turned on its head, and everything we thought to be the case isn't; everything is "topsy-turvy" (p. 236), as Miss Rehana says.

The basic plot in the comedy of reversal goes something like this: B assumes A wants X. When A refuses to take B's advice in obtaining X, all is lost. But A didn't want X after all, she wanted not-X, and the advice does help her to obtain not-X. We usually find this reversal played out as a con game, for example, when the trickster figure Brer Rabbit, from Joel Chandler Harris's Uncle Remus stories, escapes from the Tar-Baby by pleading with Brer Fox to do anything he wants to with him – including boiling, burning, and skinning him alive – just so long as the fox doesn't throw him in the briar patch. Wanting to cause the rabbit as much trouble as possible, the fox flings Brer Rabbit in the briar patch, and the rabbit, of course, is saved. "Bred en bawn in a brier-patch, Brer Fox – bred en bawn in a brier-patch!" the rabbit shouts gleefully to the fox.

In Rushdie's story, Miss Rehana isn't trying to con the con-man Ali, at least not intentionally or for financial reward, but the effect of her deception is one of comic delight in her achieving a goal the exact opposite of what the advice expert intended. Instead of a marriage comedy, Rushdie has written its reverse: a comedy of non-marriage.

Reading the Resonant Detail

Many details of Rushdie's story resonate with meaning, even seemingly trivial ones. Rushdie's prose, as readers have noticed, selects its images and references from carpets both magic and real, flown in from both the East and the West. The comma separating East from West is his preferred representative icon – "it seems to me I am that comma" (*Many Voices*, p. 324). In the sometimes playful, sometimes deadly zone between the two cultures, reside Rushdie's aesthetic energies and thematic concerns.

Consider, for example, the three written signs on the bus out of which Miss Rehana, in the opening paragraph, steps, "a cloud of dust […] veiling her beauty from the eyes of strangers". On the "bus brightly painted in multicoloured arabesques" are three signs: 1) on the front – "'MOVE OVER DARLING' in green and gold letters"; on the back 2)"TATA-BATA" and 3) "O.K. GOOD-LIFE" (p. 225). Taking these three signs one at a time – and remember that Miss Rehana tells the driver that his bus is "beautiful" – and then together, we can see an enactment of Rushdie's East / West dialectic.

Move Over, Darling, directed by Michael Gordon and starring Doris Day and James Garner, was a 1963 remake of Garson Kanin's 1940 *My Favorite Wife* with Irene Dunne and Cary Grant. The basic plot set-up is the return of a wife thought dead when in fact she's been marooned on a island with another man. In context of "Good Advice is Rarer Than Rubies" "MOVE OVER DARLING" takes part of its irony from the comedy of remarriage sub-genre and part, in this case, from the comma missing on the Bus – Move over [,] darling. In the comedy of remarriage one person wants to remarry; the other, at first, doesn't. We assume, along with Ali, that Miss Rehana wants to go to England and marry the man she's been promised to – or at least we assume so until we learn from Miss Rehana that she was nine years old when her parents arranged her marriage to Mustafa Dar, who is twenty-one years older than she (p. 235). Imagine these words, title of a remake, in this age of mechanical reproduction (Walter Benjamin), spoken by Miss Rehana, and the imperative takes on remarkable power. Move over, darling – indeed. Her darling Dar won't ever see her. In Pakistan she'll remain forever.

From a cinematic sign from the West we move to the Eastern assembly line of "TATA-BATA", an "Indian firm that makes cars and trucks not known for being of good quality", Rudolph F. Rau's note helpfully tells us. Then to the synthesis: "O.K. GOOD-LIFE" – which blends West with East in its Indian-turned English and at the same time foreshadows the story's happy ending, Miss Rehana's success in failing to get her visa. Such oxymorons (successful failure) are appropriate in a story that derives its power from reversals. "I completely redecorated, all absolutely topsy-turvy, you see", says Miss Rehana (p. 236). So, Rushdie's story suggests, should we.

Background Information: An Overview of Rushdie's Controversial *The Satanic Verses* (1988)

Published the year after "Good Advice is Rarer Than Rubies" first appeared, Rushdie's *The Satanic Verses* brought on riots, book burnings, attacks on bookstores, and deaths around the world, especially in Muslim communities, and it caused Ayatollah Ruhollah Khomeini of Iran to call for the author's murder. By writing about Mohammed the Prophet in fiction, Rushdie, according to Khomeini, had committed blasphemy.

The Satanic Verses is in the tradition of those novels that attempt with broad, inventive satire to embrace the world, or as Rushdie says, "the whole ambiguous history of east and west". Thus his tremendous range of narrative styles and reference from Lucretius to Nabokov, Apuleius to Zbigniew Herbert, *The Thousand and One Nights* to Ovid, Tagore to T. S. Eliot. And thus in this novel his emphasis on metamorphoses and mutations: "He chose Lucretius over Ovid. The inconstant soul, the mutability of everything, das Ich, every last speck. A being going through life can become so other to himself as to *be another*, discrete, severed from history." And Gabriel can become Gibreel, Aladin Saladin, Mohammed Mahound, London Babylondon.

Two Indian actors, Gibreel Farishta who portrays in Indian films "deities of every conceivable water" and Saladin Chamcha, the star of a London television fantasy entitled *The Aliens Show* and to whom "the debasing of Englishness by the English was a thing too painful to contemplate," find themselves blown out of the sky at thirty thousand feet from a hijacked plane. Together, and without parachute, they fall – and land on a snowy beach in England. For the most part the rest of the novel concerns these two fallen angels' attempts to reintegrate themselves into the world which has thought them dead. "When you've fallen from the sky," Saladin says, "been abandoned by your friend, suffered police brutality, metamorphosed into a goat, lost your work as well as your wife, learned the power of hatred and regained human shape, what is there left to do but […] demand your rights?" Gibreel's metamorphosis takes more a psychological than physical turn: he believes himself to be the angel Gabriel. Part of his delusion manifests itself in dreams, and it is these dream narratives – of Mahound the fundamentalist prophet of Jahilia, of Baal the poet and his life hiding from Mahound in a brothel, and Ayesha the orphan girl with "falling sickness" who eats butterflies and leads her villagers on a pilgrimage to the sea – that form some of the novel's richest, most moving, and controversial moments. In the novel Rushdie goes out of his way to state that this is "not history", but "a stranger dream", a novel. "Fiction is fiction", as one character says, "facts are facts." Mahound is Mahound, Mohammed Mohammed. All the rest falls under a civilization's absolute need for artistic freedom.

Rushdie's satire strikes deepest at those who believe in an unambiguous, static world, a world of only one truth. "Something was badly amiss with the spiritual life of the planet, thought Gibreel Farista. Too many demons inside people claiming to believe in God." But the religious fundamentalists aren't the only guilty ones; there is the television and film industry which prefers "style instead of substance, the image instead of the reality." Or as a Bombay film producer with a comic, signifying stutter puts it: "This picture: solid pap pap *platinum*." And there are those who have reduced the universe to its marketing potential: "In marketing parlance, a *universe* was the total potential market for a given product or service: the chocolate universe, the slimming universe." Thus "a society capable only of pastiche: a 'flattened' world." But in Rushdie's more complex view, there is always "the statement and the repudiation, verses and converses, universes and reverses." A father advises his daughter: "The world is incompatible, just never forget it: gaga. Ghosts, Nazis, saints, all alive at the same time; in one spot, blissful happiness, while down the road, the inferno. You can't ask for a wilder place."

Saladin, who will soon have to return to India and confront his own heritage and his father's death, recalls the words of another father to his sons, Henry James, Sr. to William and Henry: "Every man who has reached even his intellectual teens begins to suspect that life is not farce; that it is not genteel comedy even; that it flowers and fructifies on the contrary out of the profoundest tragic depths of the essential dearth in which its subject's roots are plunged." It is Rushdie's sense of these depths that informs his best writing, including *The Satanic Verses*, this "burlesque for our degraded, imitative times."

Teaching Suggestions

Pre-Reading Activities

1. **Find out what the students know about the history of the British Raj and its continuing influence on India and Pakistan.**
   http://en.wikipedia.org/wiki/British_Raj
   http://www.sscnet.ucla.edu/southasia/History/British/BrIndia.html

2. **Discuss Indian and Pakistani marriage customs, especially as they pertain to the story.**
   http://www.indianslivingabroad.com/matrimonial/marriage-customs.asp
   (Punjabi, Kashmiri, Kayasht and Rajput wedding customs)

While-Reading Activities

1. **As the students read the story, have them note down local colour details (clothes, food, sounds, etc.).**
   On every page of this story you'll find local colour details that supply verisimilitude and a strong sense of place. In the first two paragraphs for example we have *arabesques* and the signs on the bus, Miss Rehana's eyes absent of *antimony*, the *lala*'s *khaki* uniform and *cock-aded turban*.

2. **Note the tightness of the point of view. Does it ever shift away from Ali to another character? Is there anything in the story presented to us that Ali himself couldn't have seen or felt?**
   The opening paragraph appears to be in an omniscient third person point of view, but in the second paragraph we realize that the point of view is third person limited. We even slip into the advice expert's italicized interior thoughts on several occasions, e.g. p. 232 and p. 234.

After-Reading Activities / Analysis

1. **Why is the story told in third person from the perspective of Muhammad Ali and not Miss Rehana? What is gained by Rushdie's choice of point of view?**
   We never enter Miss Rehana's point of view. She is the story's mystery that must be solved. We know the ostensible reason why she is at the Consulate – to obtain a visa to England where her future husband awaits her – but not the real reason. By writing the story from the perspective of the advice expert, the revelation about Miss Rehana's secret will sustain the narrative tension until it is revealed to Ali and the reader. Both we and Ali are frustrated that

his advice seems not to be taken; both we and Ali are frustrated when she refuses his offer of a passport. The reversal upon which the story turns would lose its effect and purpose if the story were told from Miss Rehana's point of view. And if the story were omniscient and not limited primarily to what Ali sees and thinks, then we wouldn't be surprised at the story's turn.

2. **In the story's second sentence we're told that Miss Rehana is beautiful ("[The bus] arrived pushing a cloud of dust, veiling her beauty from the eyes of strangers until she descended" (p. 225)). Why is her beauty emphasized in the story?**

Miss Rehana's beauty casts a spell on the advice expert Muhammad Ali causing him to do something he's never done before – give advice free to a client. By instigating this first reversal, her beauty makes the rest of the story and its key reversal possible. Readers, in that they are ignorant of Miss Rehana's true desires, are as enamored and blinded as Ali. Rather than wishing to be beautiful for her future husband awaiting her in Bradford, England, Miss Rehana is not trying to use her beauty to deceive or manipulate anyone. She wants only to remain as governess, "ayah to three good boys" (p. 236). This notion of beauty suits a story where appearances are not what they seem. In the first paragraph Rushdie has already introduced (subtlely, comically) beauty as something more than a means to an end when Miss Rehana tells the bus driver that the bus is beautiful. "The bus was brightly painted in multicolored arabesques []...]. Miss Rehana told the driver it was a beautiful bus" (p. 225). It is, then, more distinctly Eastern than Western, and also (recall its verbal signs) a fusion of all three. This simple story is more multi-dimensional and arabesque, more *beautiful* (in the aesthetic sense) than it at first appears.

Topics for Class Discussion

1. **Compare and contrast Rushdie's "Good Advice is Rarer Than Rubies" to R. K. Narayan 's "A Horse and Two Goats." (See commentary on the Narayan story.)**

2. **Locate and discuss the function of the many instances of reversals in the story.**
(See above sections on "Short Summary and Interpretation" and "Narrative Structure: Reversal and Recognition".)

Creative Writing

1. **Compose a brief tale that incorporates a reversal in its plot.**

2. **Drawing from your own life, write a scene that employs specific local color details in its imagery and dialogue.**

Composition

1. **What is the story's central conflict and how is it resolved?**
   The conflict isn't what it at first seems. Rather than a story about a young woman's conflict with the British Consulate on obtaining a permit, we have a story about an advice expert in conflict with himself (should he help the woman out for free, thus abandoning his usual shady business practices?). On the social level the conflict concerns the role of women in Eastern society. The assumption by the advice expert is that she wants to follow through with the arranged marriage and go to England to be supported by her husband, when in fact she prefers to stay in Pakistan and support herself.

2. **What makes it possible for us to call this story a comedy?**
   The plot of misidentification and its consequent reversals is what makes this story a comedy. (See above section on "Narrative Structure: Reversal and Recognition".)

Topics for Presentations

1. **Present an overview of Rushdie's background and career.**
   http://www.kirjasto.sci.fi/rushdie.htm
   http://www.subir.com/rushdie.html
   http://www.contemporarywriters.com/authors/?p=auth87
   http://www.postcolonialweb.org/pakistan/literature/rushdie/rushdieov.html
   Goonetilleke, D. C. R. A. *Salman Rushdie*. New York, NY: St. Martin's, 1998.
   Cundy, Catherine. *Salman Rushdie*. Manchester, England: Manchester UP, 1996. Harrison, James. *Salman Rushdie*. New York: Twayne, 1992.

2. **Give a presentation of the concerns in Rushdie's short fiction as seen by his critics.**
   Besides the above, see the following articles:
   Rauwerda, Antje M. "East, West: Rushdie Writes Home". *South Asian Review*, 24:2, 133–48 (2003).
   Carey-Abrioux, Cynthia. "'Coming Unstuck': Salman Rushdie's Short Story 'The Courter'". In (pp. 315–22) Bardolph, Jacqueline (ed.), *Telling Stories: Postcolonial Short Fiction in English*. Amsterdam, Netherlands: Rodopi, 2001.
   Gane, Gillian. "Mixed-Up, Jumble-Aya, and English: 'How Newness Enters the World' in Salman Rushdie's 'The Courter'". *ARIEL: A Review of International English Literature*, 32:4, 47–68 (2001).
   Sen, Asha. "Allegories of Woman, Nation, and Empire in Salman Rushdie's *East, West* Stories". Kunapipi: *Journal of Postcolonial Writing,*, 23:2, 121–44 (2001).
   Beck, Rudolf. "Close Encounters of the Third Kind: Salman Rushdie's Short Story Cycle *East, West*". *Anglia: Zeitschrift für Englische Philologie*, 116:3, 355–80 (1998).
   Manferlotti, Stefano. "Salman Rushdie's Short Stories". *Textus: English Studies in Italy*, 11:1, 33–44 (1998).

Challakere, Padmaja. "Migrancy as Paranoid Schizophrenia in Salman Rushdie's *East, West*". *South Asian Review*, 20:17, 66–74 (1996).

Grant, Damian. "*East, West*: Home's Best? Salman Rushdie's Cultural Questioning". *Ateliers* 2, 33–39 (1995).

3. **Give a presentation on other Indian short story writers such as R. K. Narayan, Mulk Raj Anand, Nirad C. Chaudhuri, Saadat Hasan Manto, Nirmal Verma, O.V. Vijayan, U.R. Anantha Murthy, Ismat Chugtai, Qurratulain Hyder, Amitav Ghosh, I. Allan Sealy, Firdaus Kanga, Mukul Kesavan, Shashi Tharoor, Upamanyu Chatterjee, Ardeshir Vakil, and Kiran Desai, many of whom are included in the following two anthologies:**

New Writing in India edited by Adil Jussawalla London: Penguin, 1974.

Mirrorwork: Fifty Years of Indian Writing, 1947–1997 edited by Salman Rushdie and Elizabeth West. New York: Henry Holt, 1999.

Also see Pankaj Mishra's article/review "A Spirit of Their Own" in *The New York Review of Books* (Volume 46, Number 9 May 20, 1999).

Qaisra Shahraz
"A Pair of Jeans" (1988/2005)

Short Summary and Interpretation

The opening paragraph establishes the story's setting (north central England, near the Peak District) and principal character, Miriam, a young woman who has just returned from an outing with her university friends. From the outset special emphasis is laid on her clothes – her "jeans-clad legs" and "short vest" exposing her midriff (p. 239) as well as the emotions they provoke in her. The way Miriam feels in her clothes, however, depends upon the circumstances. Whereas she has felt comfortable in Western dress during her outing, the closer she gets to home, the more embarrassed she feels.

> Strange but she felt odd in her clothing. Yet they were just the type of clothes she needed to wear today; for hill walking in the Peak District. Somehow here, in the vicinity of her home, however, she felt different. (p. 239)

Early on suspense is created by the sentence: "She remembered the phone call of yesterday evening. They said they were coming today. What if they had already arrived?" (p. 240). She awaits them with outward signs of stress and tension – her step faltering, "colour ebbing from her face", "her heart rocking madly against her chest" (p. 240) and braces her shoulders (p. 241). For a while the reader keeps wondering who "they" are and is finally told:

> The woman was her future mother-in-law, a slightly frail woman dressed in shalwar and kameze with a chadar around her shoulders. The elderly man (...) was the woman's husband. He seemed to tower above his wife." (p. 241)

Miriam, the young woman's name as we soon learn, avoids eye contact with Ayub and Begum, her prospective parents-in-law, as they do with her. It becomes apparent that her dress is the cause of their embarrassment. "Their eyes fell straight to the inch of her waist flesh" (p. 242) The principal themes of the story – arranged marriage, clash of British and Pakistani culture and dress – are now obvious.

Fatima, Miriam's mother, is equally shocked by her daughter's clothes because she sees her through her future parents-in-law's eyes. Thus from the beginning we get to know Fatima as a person wavering between Western and traditional Pakistani values. On the one hand, she allows her daughter to wear Western clothes for an outing with her university friends, but on the other she wants her to appear in traditional Pakistani dress for her future parents-in-law.

For Ayub and Begum, however, the damage, is done and irreversible. Even Miriam's changing into "a long tunic", "baggy trousers" and "a dupatta scarf" (p. 246) to comply with Pakistani dress requirements cannot fix it. From this moment on they no longer see her as the kind, sympathetic, modest future wife of their son Farook, but as a rebellious, emancipated Westernized woman.

A mere glimpse of Miriam in Western dress is enough for Ayub to draw all kinds of conclusions, which he divulges to his wife after they have returned home:

"Do you know what she is really like? Have you thought of the effect she could have in your household? With her life style, such girls also want a lot of freedom. In fact, they want to lead their lives the way their English college friends do. Did you notice what time she came in? She knew we were coming yet that had not made any difference to her lifestyle. Do you expect her to change overnight in order to suit us? People form habits, Begum, do you understand? Are you prepared for a daughter-in-law who goes in and out of the house whenever she feels like it, dressed like that and returns home as late as that? Don't your cheeks burn at the thought of that bit of flesh you saw? Imagine how our son will feel about her! I hope shame. And what if she has a boyfriend already – have you thought of that? What if she has a boyfriend already? What if she takes drugs? What if... What if... " (p. 252)

For Ayub, Miriam's clothes trigger a series of assumptions about her character and values: a desire for freedom not compatible with the role of women in Pakistani culture, unreliability, previous relationships with other men, sensuality, etc.. Although none of Ayub's assumptions can be proven, the insecurity caused by what she wears is enough to make him stop the planned marriage. Note that Ayub's series of questions ends with a double use of the elliptical sentence "What if...?", clearly disclosing his whole tirade as mere hypothesis, yet it is still powerful enough to determine his actions.

The story exemplifies the power a person's appearance has upon others and the assumptions it can cause about that person's character, values and attitudes. It is only Miriam's clothes that make Ayub and Begum change their opinion, not anything she has said or done.

Teaching Suggestions

Pre-Reading Activities

1. Questionnaire

Initiate a talk with the class about clothes and make-up in general. Start off with the students' personal experiences, have them talk about when they wear what, how much money they spend on clothes, etc.. Then hand out the questionnaire and have them fill it out in pairs. Each student interviews his or her partner and jots down the answers. Then some students present their partners' attitudes towards clothes. These presentations may then be commented on by the other students or the teacher, thus triggering off a class discussion on this topic.

Alternative: Collect all the questionnaires and have some students calculate the percentages and make a graph of the class's attitude towards clothes for homework. You may want to distinguish between boys and girls. The students then present their findings in the next lesson.

2. Discussion

'Clothes make the man' versus 'Wearing a cowl doesn't make one a monk'

In a second step have the students talk about the importance of clothes in general. You may want to start off a discussion about the title of Gottfried Keller's novella Kleider machen Leute (Clothes make the man or: Fine feathers make fine birds.) and compare it with its opposite: "Eine Kutte macht noch keinen Mönch" (Wearing a cowl[1] doesn't make one a monk.),

Alternative: Have the class form two groups and initiate a debate. The first half collects arguments supporting the first proverb, the second half collects arguments sustaining the second one. Then the debate starts and each group has to defend their point of view.

3. Transparency

a) Compare the two outfits. In which parts of the world are they worn?

Picture one shows a Pakistani woman dressed in shalwar[2] and kameze[3]. Draped over her right shoulder is a chadar[4]. This is the traditional dress of Muslim women in India and Pakistan.

Picture two depicts a woman in fashionable Western outfit – tight jeans with ultra-low waist and extremely short shirt exposing her midriff. Nowadays, in our globalized world, women all over the world adhering to Western values are dressed like this.

b) What do those two types of outfit reveal about the society's attitude towards the female body?

The traditional dress of a Muslim woman in picture one conceals rather than exposes a woman's body. Female curves are evened out by the loose-fitting nature of the dress and body parts associated with sexuality are hidden beneath ample layers of clothing. In Muslim society women ideally have to correspond to the ideal of being sharif, the Arabic word for modest and virtuous. Consequently, the female body is perceived as something that you do not show off to anybody.

The Western dress in picture two, however, underscores rather than hides the beauty of the female body. The tight-fitting jeans, the short shirt exposing the midriff and the low neckline accentuate the wearer's body. The female form is perceived as something that you can be proud of and have every right to show off.

c) Think of pros and cons both types of outfit imply for their wearers.

On the one hand, the traditional Pakistani dress does not allow women to show their bodies in the same way Western clothes would allow them to do and therefore constitutes a restriction of their freedom. On the other hand, however, it imbues its wearers with respect since men's attention is not immediately drawn to a woman's corporal beauty. Thus, one might argue, the perception of her character and her personality is not obstructed through too much focus on her superficial beauty. Furthermore, attention is drawn to her face rather than her body.

Western dress emphasizing the female shape allows women to take pride in their bodies. Some people might, however, object that this kind of dress reduces women to sex objects and thus focuses too much on their outward appearance instead of allowing others to appreciate their inner values.

However, one must not forget that in Western society, women can decide freely what they want to wear and opt for more loose-fitting clothes, although among youngsters peer pressure is often so strong that most teenagers bow to the latest fashion trends (comparable in some ways, then, to how Muslim women often have to adhere to a dress code).

Western fashion also exerts pressure on women whose bodies do not conform to the "ideal". Perhaps an overweight Muslim woman suffers less since in shalwar and kameze or a sari her body shape is concealed to a much higher degree. Also anorexia is less common in less Westernized countries, a fact showing the downside of our obsession with slenderness.

While-Reading Activity

Anticipating how the story continues...
Have the students read the story up to the appearance of Ayub and Begum (up to page 241, line 6: "Their eyes fell straight to the inch of her waist flesh") Then have them guess what might happen.
– Who are "they"?
– What might be reasons why the young girl is so upset about meeting ,them'?

After-Reading Activities

1. **Narrator and Point of View**
   Take a close look at the story. From whose point of view is it told?
   Whereas the first half of the story is told from Miriam's point of view (p. 239 to 249, l. 10), the second half is at first told from Begum's point of view (p. 249. l. 11 to p. 259, l. 6), but then turns to Miriam's perspective again with the sentence: "Miriam had just got in from university when she heard the phone ringing" (p. 259, l. 7) and remains like this until the end (p. 262, l. 10). The alternative ending to the story is told from Miriam's perspective as well.

Thus the reader is able to see the plot from two different perspectives – the young woman's point of view, who, being part of British society as well, suffers from the strict Pakistani traditions, and through the middle-aged woman's eyes – trying to enforce those same traditions without really being convinced either, but merely acting out the role her husband and Pakistani conventions prescribe for her. Thus we get to know typical attitudes of first- and second-generation Pakistani immigrants towards Western as well as their native culture.

2. Change of dress – change of personality
Try to find out how Miriam's clothes and her behaviour are interrelated.
How does wearing a shalwar kameze suit change Miriam?
In order to please her future parents-in law and to repair the damage caused by her not complying with Pakistani dress requirements, Miriam changes into a traditional Pakistani outfit

> "From her wardrobe she pulled off a blue crepe shalwar kameze suit from a hanger. As she put it on, her rebellious spirit reared its head again. "They are only clothes!" her mind hissed in anger.
> She could not deny the fact, however, that in having them on her back she had embraced a new set of values; in fact a new personality. Her body was now modestly swathed in an elegant tunic and baggy trousers. The curvy contours of her body were discreetly draped. With a quick glance in the mirror she left her room. It was a confident woman gliding down the stairs. She was now in full control of herself. There was to be no scuttling down the stairs. Her poise was back. (p. 246)

As soon as she has changed into her Pakistani clothes, Miriam becomes an entirely different person. Her gait and her whole attitude change. She is aware of this change herself and is very critical of it.

> "Once outside in the hallway, outside the sitting room door, she halted, her own hypocrisy galling her. She was neatly acting out a role, the one her in-laws preferred" (p. 246)

Note that not only her perception of herself changes with the dress she wears, but also her gait. Instead of scuttling down the stairs as she would have in a pair of jeans, in which she has also "traipsed" (p. 247) the countryside of the Peak District, she now glides down the stairs in style and enters the living room, her "head held high" (p. 247). (The alliteration at this point further underscores her elegant appearance.)

> "It was amazing how she was able to move around the room in her shalwar kameze suit, in a manner that she could never have done in her earlier clothes amongst these people." (p. 247)

3. Gender Relations

Characterize the relationship between Begum and Ayub, Miriam's future in-laws.
When Begum and Ayub first appear, we immediately see that Ayub is the dominant one in the relationship. "He seemed to tower above his wife." (p. 241) Begum, on the other hand, is seen submissively, "silently walking behind her husband" (p. 242)

Later in the story a sort of mutual agreement is reached by not talking about things. Tradition clearly defines what they are supposed to do or not to do. So there is less need to talk or argue about things than with Western couples. After their visit to Fatima's and Miriam's house they walk to their car "in silence" and the "silence" continues "during their journey". "There was no need for communication". They have been together for so long that they are able to guess what the other is "thinking about and read each other's thoughts fairly accurately." (p. 249)

When, however, they get home and her husband calls Begum, "his voice supremely auto-cratic" (p. 250), it becomes even more apparent that Ayub is the dominant person of their re-lationship – the one who really decides. His domineering nature is underlined by his outward appearance, namely "the harsh outlines" of his "unsmiling face" as well as his voice, which is described as "cutting" (p. 251).

Their conversation is very indirect. They never really raise their voices. There always seems to be a sort of tacit agreement between them. Nevertheless, it is obvious that Ayub is in charge of the decisions. However, he does not give orders to his wife in an authoritative, direct way. On the contrary, she has to guess his feelings and thoughts and then act accordingly – a very subtle, but extremely effective way for Ayub to get what he wants.

Begum appears unsure of herself:

> "She wanted to excuse Miriam's mode of dress to herself and to him; she knew she was not going to make a success of it because, secretly in her own heart, she very much agreed with her husband" (p. 252)

Although she seems to like Miriam and knows that her son Farook fancies her too, she finally bows to both her husband and Pakistani tradition, knowing that it is no use opposing them. It is out of the question to disagree openly with her husband.

A little later, Ayub explains the role Pakistani women have to play within marriage.

> "You know of a number of cases where the educated, the so-called modern girls have twined their husbands around their little fingers, and expected them to dance to their tunes. Are you prepared for that to happen to your beloved son? To lose him to such a daughter-in-law? (p. 253)

To him there is no question that Pakistani women have to be subordinate to their husbands. He considers it an outrage if a man ever bows to their opinion. To him a relationship does not mean that each one bows to the other under certain circumstances, so that an equilibrium can be maintained; it is clear that the man is the one who decides and that any man who does what his wife wants him to do is to be pitied.

Begum completely corresponds to that role in their conversation, anticipating her husband's opinion and then acting accordingly:

> "She had already jumped ahead. With a sinking heart, she had guessed correctly the conclusion, the outcome of his discussion. She did not know how to react in front of him, nor did she disagree with him over anything he said. Not one jot. " (pp. 254–255)

Ironically, it is Begum who has to break the unpleasant news of the wedding cancellation to the other family and not Ayub, although it was he who made the decision. (cf. p. 258)

Topics for Class Discussion

1. **You and your other self**
   - Do you sometimes change roles according to who you are with?
   - Does playing a certain role under certain circumstances inevitably mean that you are not true to yourself?
   - Should an honest person always show his or her true self?
   - Is there such a thing as a true self at all or is the way you are always influenced by your environment – the people you are with or the setting you find yourself in?

2. **Living in two worlds – switching roles**
   Miriam lives in two worlds switching roles along with her dress.
   - Is it stressful for her to do justice to those two worlds?
   - Where does she glide from one world to the other rather smoothly?
   - Where is a smooth transition no longer possible, revealing a clash of cultures?

   Through a change of dress Miriam becomes "the other self". Have you ever had an experience like that? Do you think you can change into someone else by wearing something else? ad. lib.

   Students might argue that by wearing a certain outfit not you yourself change, but the way your environment perceives you is definitely altered, which again might have repercussions on the way you feel.

3. **Comparison of the two endings**
   - Which ending do you like better? Give reasons for your answer.
   ad. lib.

   - **Which ending do you consider to be more likely?**
   ad. lib.

   - **Do you think it is a good idea to offer the reader two endings?**
     On the one hand it makes the reader think and makes him aware of the process of writing (makes him realize that there is not just one ending from the beginning, but that writers alter the plot as they write), but on the other hand it doesn't satisfy the urge of many readers to know the outcome, to learn what "really happened".

Creative Writing

1. Farook – the invisible person
Farook is mentioned, but does not appear in the first version of the story. Make up a fictional biography for him and choose pictures from magazines that you think might resemble him. Then read the second ending to "A Pair of Jeans" and compare Farook as you imagined him to the person created by Shahraz.

2. Personification of the jeans in the first ending

> "The vest and shabby-looking and much worn pair of jeans lay nonchalantly near the end of the bed, blissfully unaware of the havoc they had created in the life of their wearer" (p. 262)

In this passage Shahraz personifies an object – the vest and the pair of jeans. Go a step further now. Imagine the jeans have a life of their own and start to speak. What would they say? Make up an interior monologue in which the jeans begin to speak..... You may want to add narrative sections to give the story a strange or absurd twist.

ad. lib.

Topics for Presentations

1. Pakistan – a country of contrasts
Do a presentation on Pakistan. Try to give your classmates a general impression of this country (geography, politics, religion). You may also want to focus on the role women play in this society. The following web sites might be helpful:
http://www.tourism.gov.pk/
http://www.cia.gov/cia/publications/factbook/geos/pk.html
http://www.infopak.gov.pk/
http://www.jang.com.pk/
http://www.pakistanlink.com/

2. Arranged marriage
Do research on arranged marriages in Pakistan as well as among Pakistani immigrants in Great Britain. You may want to go to the following web sites:
http://news.bbc.co.uk/1/hi/uk/1809791.stm
http://news.bbc.co.uk/2/hi/south_asia/3191827.stm
http://www.deccanherald.com/deccanherald/july252004/fp4.asp
http://www.burr.kent.edu/archives/2001/spring/marriage/marriage1.html
http://www.members.aol.com/ruqaiyyah/articles/arrangedm.htm

A QUESTIONNAIRE – Clothes and You

1. **How important are clothes for you?**
   a) Essential. I spend a lot of time thinking about what to wear before I go out and spend a major portion of my pocket money on my outfit.
   b) Average. On special occasions I select my clothes very carefully. Other than that I don't spend too much thought or money on what I wear.
   c) Of minor Importance. I don't care what I wear as long as it doesn't look completely dorky.
   d) For me, above all, clothes have to be functional. In the summer they have to be cool, in the winter warm. I don't understand all the fuss people make about their outfit. How can people torment themselves wearing high heels or freeze themselves to death in ultra-short sweaters exposing their midriff in the wintertime just because it is fashionable?

2. **Do you wear different clothes on different occasions?**
   a) I usually wear pretty much the same things day in, day out. I just dress up if I have to.
   b) I select my outfit very carefully according to the occasion. Every time I go out I think about whom I will meet, what the others will probably wear, and choose my clothes accordingly.
   c) "I am what I am!" I do not let other people dictate to me what to wear on certain occasions. I have my own style of dress. I would never change my outfit to match the occasion!

3. **What do you think about people who are not dressed very fashionably?**
   a) I feel sorry for them. Don't they have the money to buy proper clothes?
   b) I can't understand that they don't give any thought to their outfit. For me what you wear is a way of making certain statements about yourself, of ascertaining who you are and what impression of yourself you want to convey.
   c) I don't care what other people wear. Their personality is more important to me.
   d) I usually don't even remember what people wear. I recall people's faces and voices, but most of the time wouldn't be able to tell you what they wore after meeting them.

4. **Have you ever felt awkward because you were not wearing the proper clothes?**
   a) No, never. I've never felt out of place because of my clothes.
   b) Yes, I remember occasions where I felt awkward because I was underdressed.
   c) Yes, I remember occasions where I felt awkward because I was overdressed.
   d) I don't care what other people think of me. I always wear what I consider to be right, no matter what the occasion.

5. **In your opinion, how much does what one wears reveal about a person?**
   a) Not very much. I think there is no correlation between clothes and personality.
   b) The way a person dresses says a lot about his or her status in society. You can see from somebody's clothes which job he or she has and how much money he or she earns.
   c) Depends. Sometimes clothes say a lot about a person; at other times, they don't, and you are surprised at what the person is really like.
   d) I think clothes say a lot about a person's values or moral attitudes. If I see a person for the first time, I can immediately say whether they are rather conservative, religious, progressive, right- or left-wing.

6. **Clothes and first impressions – How important do you consider a person's clothes in forming your first impressions of him or her?**
   a) of utmost importance
   b) fairly important
   c) not very important
   d) not important at all. Other things, say much more about people than what they wear.

Copymaster

ADDITIONAL MATERIAL
A Pair of Jeans by Qaisra Shahraz
An Analysis by the Author, in Terms of Style, Context and Language

The use of body language and clothes is very important in A Pair of Jeans. Clothes are symbolic in the context in which they are used. Their relationship with the wearer is the focus of attention and analysis. They directly influence the psychological state of mind of the young woman. The contrast between what she feels before she enters her home and after she meets the in-laws is the crux of this relationship. She is more comfortable in the latter clothes on the home ground. In the outside world jeans make her feel carefree and she is not inhibited by them. They definitely do not 'burn' her. In this context they are just ordinary articles of clothing. While she feels comfortable in jeans outside, she is more comfortable in traditional clothes at home. They show that her two worlds are divided by her clothing – her home and the world outside. Normally she weaves in naturally between the two worlds, in the appearance of the in-laws, her two worlds have clashed and her discomfort is very obvious.

The clothes have taken on a larger than life role. They swamp her and she becomes very conscious of them, of her appearance, how her body is tightly encased in them. They show off her body, probably in a bad, seductive light. The realisation, as it hits Miriam, is what brings on the change in her relationship with her clothes. She is wearing the wrong clothes in the wrong place, and seen by the wrong people. It is almost a displacement of her personality.

They are the wrong ones, presenting her in the wrong context – in fact the wrong cultural context. They alienate her from herself as much as they alienate her in-laws. It is this alienation and her unease at being seen in them and the cultural value that is attached to them: western decadence and female immodesty which alters her relationship with the article of clothing.

Now the jeans have become 'a silly pair of jeans' and the jacket is 'ridiculous'. Finally at the end her clothes even lose their names. The jeans become the 'repugnant looking article' and lead to her downfall.

The whole thing is completely turned around from being at home in them she is now revolted by them. They have brought on that cultural alienation in her mind and also led to what has apparently happened.

Her mother also experiences a feeling of unease, a similar pattern of behaviour, although on a smaller scale to her daughter. She too, although used to her daughter wearing such clothes everyday, today she feels uncomfortable and wants to 'usher' her daughter out of sight. Her actions and the tempo of the relationship with the other party are dictated by her unease of knowing and witnessing the reaction of the in-laws to her daughter's appearance.

Words are repeated for effect. Emphasis is placed in body language, facial features i.e. 'the pinched look around Fatima's mouth', 'sound in her head' – to focus on the psychological state of mind of the people.

There is parallelism – both the mothers feel the unease – both victims. As they know that the relationship is breaking down, but they are helpless to do anything. Words like 'as in a daze', 'to burst out with', later 'why, why' indicate the state of Miriam's mind – shock, rebellion, anger and the need to know more. She feels she has been victimised and wants to fight back, when she has recovered herself and built up her own self confidence.

Miriam's father has no role in the story. He is conveniently absent. It is the relationship of the three women with each other and with the father-in-law, that is the driving force in the story. Another man would have taken away that tension.

The focus on the clash of culture is emphasised by the sentence 'her friends would never believe her' for she has gone through a cultural metamorphosis that only she can identify with. They can't. They are not part of the cultural package and therefore they will not be able to understand or appreciate the situation. Compared to the psychological turbulence in Miriam's life, the pair of jeans is an inanimate object and has no idea of what 'havoc' it causes – i.e. is thus 'blissfully unaware' of what is going on and lies 'nonchalantly' on the floor.

Her rejection of the jeans and her anger at what they have caused is conveyed by her throwing it out on the floor.

The relationship between the father-in-law and the mother-in-law is highlighted by the repetitive use of words like 'silence', 'Begum pretended'. They are playing a game with each other. They know each other's minds but Begum is trying to fight on Miriam's behalf, but with not much success. Her husband aggressively overrides that. His dominance in his relationship with his wife ensures that he has his way. It is his decision that is the final one. His wife is only left with regret and silent rebellion.

The story is told by the omniscient narrator, because the writer prefers this mode of writing, analysing the event from a detached of point of view.

Hanif Kureishi
"My Son the Fanatic" (1994)

Interpretation and Background Information

Short Summary and Interpretation

Similar to classical Greek drama, the story consists of five sections and follows the model of Freitag's triangle (exposition – rising action / complication – climax – falling action / turning point (peripeteia) / delaying factor – resolution / catastrophe). The first section (p. 272, l. 1 – p. 274, l. 11) describes Ali's change from an untidy teenager playing the guitar, owning many computer and video games and having an English girlfriend to a spartanically living youngster getting rid of all his possessions and breaking off with his former lover. It serves as the exposition of the short story, introducing the two main characters, Ali and his father Parvez, a Punjabi taxi driver in England, as well as presenting the incipient conflict – the son's change and his father's bewilderment about it.

In the second part (p. 274, l. 12 – p. 277, l. 6) Parvez, searching for help, reveals his mystification about his son's behaviour to his colleagues. When his fellow taxi drivers suspect that Ali is taking drugs, Parvez begins to search his son's possessions for clues – a sign that, already at this point of the story, an open conversation between father and son is no longer possible and the only way Parvez thinks he can get to know what his son is up to is by spying on him. This part constitutes the rising action, in which suspense is created by the fact that Parvez is looking for answers to explain his son's metamorphosis, but is not able to find them yet.

In the third section (p. 277, l. 7 – p. 279, l. 8) the explanation for Ali's striking change is found – Parvez's son has turned extremely religious, prays five times a day and follows all other rules of the Koran by the letter, which explains why he throws out his possessions and gets rid of his Western girlfriend. The fact that Parvez now knows that extreme devotion to the Muslim faith is the reason for his son's heretofore inexplicable transformation determines the further steps he takes, thus influencing the outcome of the story. Parvez's revelation can be seen as the story's climax.

Told in flashback at one of Parvez's meetings with Bettina, the fourth section (p. 279, l. 10 – p. 285, l. 3) details the conversation between father and son at a restaurant in which their different attitudes towards religion and, in a more general sense, the way one should live one's life clash. This constitutes the height of the verbal conflict, the turning point or peripeteia of the story, where it becomes obvious that the differences between father and son are insurmountable. Reaching an agreement or simply understanding each other will from now on no longer be possible. This is already hinted at by Parvez's remark: *"I'm going to tell him to pick up his prayer mat and get out of my house. It will be the hardest thing I've ever done, but tonight I'm going to do it."* (p. 284). This section therefore does not merely constitute the falling action, but also serves as a delaying factor postponing the final catastrophe that, at this point of the story, can no longer be avoided.

The fifth section (p. 285, l. 5 – p. 288, l. 26) shows the final confrontation between father and son ending in violence. After Ali has insulted his father's girlfriend Bettina because she is a prostitute,

Parvez is no longer able to accept his son's religious fervour and, after having had a couple of drinks, goes up to his room and beats him. His son stoically accepts blow after blow, neither protecting himself nor retaliating, but just asks: *So who's the fanatic now?* (p. 288), thereby revealing his father – and, in a more general way, the West – to be at least as fanatic as himself.

Point of View

All the events in the story are presented from Parvez's point of view. We get to know his thoughts and feelings in detail – from his initial confusion about Ali's behaviour to his certain knowledge about his son's fanaticism and his subsequent anger and rage. Thus Kureishi at first glance gives us a very one-sided account of the action. Only at the very end is the father's attitude put into question, namely when his son asks him: *"So who's the fanatic now?"* (p. 288) In retrospect, this single sentence changes the reader's perception of the whole story. Whereas up to that point, the reader has tended to see things from Parvez's point of view, that is a Western perspective, he now needs to adjust his view and reevaluate the story. Suddenly it is no longer clear who is more fanatic – father or son?

Teaching Suggestions

Pre-Reading Activity

Speculating About a Quotation

"I can't understand it! (...) Everything is going from his room. And I can't talk to him any more. We were not father and son – we were brothers! Where has he gone? Why is he torturing me?" (p. 274)

Write this quotation from the story on the board.

First talk about it by asking:
– Who is speaking here?
– What is the speaker complaining about?

Then have the students guess:
– What might be reasons for the conflict hinted at in this quotation?

While-Reading Activities

1. **Reading the Opening Paragraphs of the Story**
   Have the students read the opening paragraphs of the story (up to p. 274, l. 19).
   Make them guess about possible reasons for Ali's behaviour.

2. **Contrast Ali's old lifestyle with his new one.**

Ali's old lifestyle	Ali's new lifestyle
– untidy (His bedroom used to be a tangle of clothes, books, cricket bats and video games.) – used to have an English girlfriend who came to the house – used to have many friends – used to play the guitar – owned a TV, a video-player and a stereo system	– neat and orderly – gives away new books, computer disks, videotapes, fashionable clothes – has broken up with his English girlfriend – is no longer in touch with his old friends – has developed a sharp tongue – no longer plays his guitar, gives it away – throws out his TV, video-player and stereo system – has taken down all the pictures in his room

1. The story ends with a question: "So who's the fanatic now?" (p. 288). Answer this question with respect to the story.

Up until the end of the story we can probably answer this question without hesitation by saying: Of course, Ali is the fanatic. He is a fundamentalist who is ready to use violence for the sake of Islam. To him Islam offers the one and only truth and he therefore clearly opposes Western values – at least he says he would be ready to use violence if he continues to feel oppressed by the West. He speaks of *jihad* and accuses the West of being "a sink of hypocrites, adulterers, homosexuals, drug users and prostitutes" (p. 282).

In the very last paragraph of the story, however, our perception changes. Parvez, no longer able to suppress his feelings of anger and rage after having had a couple of drinks, goes up to his son's bedroom and hits him continuously, not even stopping when Ali's face is already covered in blood. His son, however, neither protects nor defends himself, but stoically accepts one blow after the other. Suddenly the father is the intolerant one, the one who and isn't able to accept that his son has a different world view, but needs to resort to violence to prove him wrong.

2. What does Bettina mean to Parvez? Find passages in the text that throw light on the nature of their relationship.

Although, unlike the two main characters, Bettina is not mentioned in the story's exposition, Kureishi introduces her fairly early in the second part – long before Parvez's wife has been mentioned.

> Bettina had known Parvez for three years. She lived outside the town and, on the long drives home, during which she sat not in the passenger seat but beside him, Parvez had talked to her about his life and hopes, just as she talked about hers. They saw each other most nights. (p. 275)

There is a lot of confidentiality between them. Parvez *"could talk to her about things he'd never be able to discuss with his own wife"* (p. 275) and that is the reason why he tells her about his son's sudden change. Unlike his colleagues, Bettina does not just assume that Ali takes drugs, but tells Parvez to watch his son closely, adding that: *"It's all in the eyes."* (p. 276) Bettina and Parvez also frequently meet in a romantic setting:

> They drove out across the moors and parked at the spot where, on better days, their view unimpeded for miles except by wild deer and horses, they'd lie back, with their eyes half-closed, saying, "This is the life." (p. 279)

Later, as Parvez tells her about the disappointing dinner with Ali, in which his son has castigated him for drinking alcohol and eating pork, *she puts her arms around him* and *rubs his head* (p. 279) and when they pick up Ali, who has been to a mosque in a poor district of town, *she inadvertently lays her hand on Parvez's shoulder* (p. 287). Although Kureishi never explicitly says that Bettina and Parvez are lovers, these gestures and the familiarity with which they talk about private issues as well as the regularity of their meetings at night clearly suggest a love affair.

Topics for Class Discussion

1. Breakdown of communication

Ali and Parvez are not able to communicate with each other openly. That is why Parvez spies on his son and searches his possessions. Have you ever been in a situation where you felt that the only way of getting to know something about somebody else was to spy on him / her or search his possessions because you were no longer able to have an open talk with him / her?

ad. lib.

Similarly, in the end, father and son are no longer able to speak with each other, but violence takes over. Can you think of similar situations (maybe situations you have come across in the news or in another story or in your life) where you or somebody else have resorted to violence because communication had failed?

ad. lib.

Creative Writing

First-person-narrative from Ali's point of view

Choose the passage from the story you consider to be most important (Indicate its page numbers and lines). Reread it and then rewrite it from Ali's point of view. Use a first-person-narrator.

Dramatization

Reread the fourth section of the short story (pp. 279 – 285). In this part Kureishi informs us about the dinner between father and son in a flashback (as Parvez tells Bettina about it the next day). Turn this section into a scene for a play. Then act it out.

Composition

1. Compare Qaisra Shahraz's "A Pair of Jeans" to Hanif Kureishi's "My Son the Fanatic". Pay special attention to the attitudes parents and children assume towards their native Muslim culture and the more liberal, Western society they live in.

When comparing "A Pair of Jeans" to "My Son the Fanatic", it becomes obvious that first and second generation immigrants, or, to put it another way, parents and children, can assume completely different attitudes towards the values of their native Muslim culture and those of the Western society they live in.

Whereas in "A Pair of Jeans" the first generation of immigrants (Ayub, Begum and Fatima) stick more or less to traditional Muslim values – in this case modest clothing for women – and the second generation (Miriam) demand more freedom and tolerance – being able to wear Western dress, for example, in Kureishi's story the roles of parents and children have been reversed. It is Ali, the son, who lives a very strict, almost fanatic religious life – praying five times a day, getting rid of everything that is connected with the West – his guitar, his CDs and, most shockingly, his English girlfriend. He even goes so far as to develop a missionary attitude and is convinced that there is only one truth, one way to live by, one religion that can save the world – Islam. When they meet at the restaurant for dinner, he tells his father so in no uncertain terms:

> The law of Islam would rule the world; the skin of the infidel would burn off again and again; the Jews and Christers would be routed. The West was a sink of hypocrites, adulterers, homosexuals, drug users and prostitutes. (p. 282)

What is really shocking about Ali, however, is not that he decides to live his life according to the values of the Koran, but that he speaks of *jihad* and says that Western civilization has to be fought:

> My people have taken enough. If the persecution doesn't stop, there will be jihad. I, and millions of others, will gladly give our lives for the cause. (p. 282)

With this remark Ali no longer distinguishes himself from the suicide bombers who are willing to kill themselves for the sake of their faith. It is no wonder that this remark makes Parvez cry and he feels as if he has lost his son (cf. pp. 283 and 284).
From this moment on it is clear that Ali aggressively opposes the values of the West and is ready to use violence to fight for his belief if necessary.
It is no wonder that Ali's attitude leads to an open confrontation with his father, who has completely assimilated a Western lifestyle. Parvez drinks alcohol, eats pork and possibly has sexual relationships with the prostitutes like his colleagues do (*"A ride in exchange for a ride, it was called";* p. 275) although he is married. Furthermore he has an affair with Bettina, one of the prostitutes whose clothes are everything but modest or *sharif*:

> The next day, Parvez went immediately to the street corner where Bettina stood in the rain wearing high heels, a short skirt, and a long mac, which she would open hopefully at passing cars. (p. 279)

Parvez does not reject Western dress, and, by extension, liberal moral attitudes, as strict Muslims would (cf. Begum and Ayub in "A Pair of Jeans"). In fact, he does not even seem to notice that there is a clash of values between his strict Muslim upbringing and Bettina's clothes. Only when his son Ali gets into his taxi, does Parvez realize that Bettina's dress does not correspond to Muslim dress requirements for women (just like in "A Pair of Jeans" Fatima only becomes aware of her daughter Miriam's Western clothes when she sees her through her prospective parents-in-law's lenses):

> "Parvez became aware of Bettina's short skirt, her gaudy rings and ice-blue eyeshadow. He became conscious that the smell of her perfume, which he loved, filled the cab. He opened the window." (p. 287)

Whereas "A Pair of Jeans" lives up to the readers' expectations that children tend to be less conservative than their parents and often rebel against the traditional set of values their elders try to imbue them with, "My Son the Fanatic" thwarts our expectations by showing us that young people in their search for values and guidelines for their life in a complicated world, can have much more traditional, albeit fundamentalist attitudes than their elders. At the same time this story gives us an insight into the (psychological) reasons why the fundamentalist Islamic revival around the globe attracts so many young Muslims who have grown up in the West. (cf. Kureishi's essay "Why Fanaticism?", pp. 328–334)

2. Criticism of religion

Similar to Spark's story "The Black Madonna", which attacks the hypocrisy of many Catholics, Hanif Kureishi's "My Son the Fanatic" throws a rather critical light on religion. Find passages in "My Son the Fanatic" where Kureishi hints at the hypocrisy of many Muslims or criticizes some aspects of this faith, such as oppression of its members and intolerance towards other beliefs.

Similar to Spark's story the hypocrisy of religion is mentioned in Kureishi's story as well, albeit only in an aside and not nearly in such a sarcastic and poignant way as in "The Black Madonna":

> Not that the other taxi-drivers had any more respect than he. In fact, they made jokes about the local mullahs walking around with their caps and beards, thinking they could tell people how to live while their eyes roved over the boys and girls in their care. (p. 278)

Both the father's and the son's attitude towards the Muslim faith are revealed in the course of the story and both reveal critical aspects of religion. Whereas Parvez has a negative and oppressive memory of Muslim religion from when he grew up in Lahore, Pakistan and where he was forced to pray for hours,

> Parvez had grown up in Lahore, where all young boys had been taught the Koran. To stop Parvez from falling asleep while he studied, the maulvi had attached a piece of string to the ceiling and tied it to Parvez's hair, so if his head fell forward, he would instantly jerk awake. After this indignity, Parvez had avoided all religions. (p. 278)

to his son Ali religion seems to offer salvation. *"For us, the reward will be in Paradise"* (p. 282), he claims, and he believes that by respecting the rules of the Koran, he will get there. Ali does not feel valued by the society he lives in. *"The Western materialists hate us,"* (p. 282) he claims and is willing to resort to violence to prove them wrong. Since it is a fundamentalist attitude and since it is openly aggressive towards other religions, it throws a negative light on the missionary fervour of many religions that has caused so much suffering for so many centuries. To Parvez he sounds *"as if he'd swallowed someone else's voice."* (p. 283). He no longer recognizes his son in what comes from his lips. Kureishi thereby criticizes the brainwashing effect religion may have.

3. Compare the father-son relationship in "My Son the Fanatic" to the mother-daughter relationship in "A Pair of Jeans"

Whereas the female characters play the main part in Qaisra Shahraz's "A Pair of Jeans" (Miriam's father is completely left out and Farook only appears in the second version), "My Son the Fanatic" centers on the relationship between father and son. The female characters – Parvez's wife and his lover Bettina – are of minor importance. Ali's mother is hardly mentioned at all and does not even have a name, but is simply referred to as Parvez's wife (p. 277). Although Bettina is portrayed in much more detail, she is not nearly as important as father and son. From the outset it is clear that the relationship between father and son is one of the main themes of Kureishi's story. The word "son" is already part of the title and both words father and son are used in one sentence at the beginning of the story, when Parvez is looking for reasons to explain his son's change of behaviour.

> "I can't understand it!(...) Everything is going from his room. And I can't talk to him any more. We were not father and son – we were brothers!" (p. 274)

When the culture gap between the two lies wide open, Parvez makes one last effort at reconciliation by inviting his son for dinner and again uses both words – father and son – when explaining to Ali why this date is of utmost importance: *"Parvez had to insist that no appointment could be more important than that of a son with his father."* (p. 279)
In the course of their dinner at the restaurant, however, the roles of father and son are reversed. It is the son who castigates the father and disapproves of his behaviour, thus assuming the superior part in their conversation.

> "Each time Parvez took a drink, the boy winced or made some kind of fastidious face."
> (p. 280)

At another point of their dinner, when Ali informs him about his conviction that Islam should rule the world, he addresses him *"as if Parvez were a rowdy crowd which had to be quelled or convinced"* (p. 282)
The mother-daughter relationship in "A Pair of Jeans" is of an entirely different nature. The interaction between Fatima and Miriam is part and parcel of the story, but never laid special emphasis on. Moreover, it is much more harmonious. There is no open confrontation, but from the start there seems to be a tacit agreement between them. Never do they oppose each other openly. Fatima is only shocked at her daughter's clothes because she sees her through her prospective parents-in-law's eyes, not because she herself has a problem with Miriam wearing Western clothes. Both Miriam and Fatima are one hundred percent at home in both cultures. In the second version of the story, Fatima in the end even supports her daughter's decision to meet Farook, thereby taking over her daughter's attitude and adapting her own world view to modern times and learning from her daughter's experiences.

> Pakistan was so far from Britain. It was another place, and she was thinking of another time. As her daughter had said, it wasn't a matter of what was the right thing to do conventionwise, but it was time for positive action. If Miriam thought she had a right to consult Farook about this matter, then she had every right to do so, and she, as her mother, would support her! Times had indeed changed. (p. 267)

Suggestions for Including Hanif Kureishi's Article "Why Fanaticism?" (pp. 328–334)

Short Summary and Interpretation

In this piece Kureishi tries to examine why in liberal, Western European countries like England, France or Germany so many second and third-generation immigrants turn to fundamentalist restrictive and authoritarian Muslim beliefs denying them pleasures and liberties – such as sex, music, alcohol, friendship and moving out – many teenagers have fought hard to achieve.

His answer is that in a time where *"ancient hierarchies have been broken down"* (p. 330), a time where there are no longer any norms and values, many young people desperately seek guidelines for their life. Strict adherence to the Muslim faith takes the burden of freedom off their shoulders and offers them a way out of their spiritual malaise.

Teaching Suggestions

Pre-Reading Activity

Fish bowl (cf. copymaster)
Divide the class into three groups. Then, hand out one role card to each group. Have each group read and discuss the role cards and find pros and cons for their position. It is advisable to encourage them to take notes. (Allow about ten minutes for this.)
Then place three chairs in front of the class. Designate one speaker for each group. Have the three speakers sit down on the chairs and read out their role cards. Then the discussion starts and, while staying in role, each of the three students tries to find arguments for the opinion on his or her role card. Then a fourth chair is added on which anybody from the class may decide to sit down to ask the other three students questions or comment on their statements. In a second round, students may then also stand behind the chairs of the three people with the role cards and find arguments in favour of their position, so that the whole class can participate in the debate in an ordered framework.

Topic for Class Discussion

The arrogance of the West
"The West had no idea of its own arrogance, and was certainly not concerned about the extent to which it had no interest in anything outside itself." (pp. 330–331)
Discuss this statement from Kureishi's text. Think about how much we really know about Muslim culture in our country. Do you consider our society to be arrogant towards the East?
ad. lib.

Topic for Presentation

Prepare a presentation on Islamic fundamentalism. The following websites might be helpful.
http://en.wikipedia.org/wiki/Islamic_fundamentalism
http://encarta.msn.com/encyclopedia_701505583/Fundamentalism_Islamic.html

Role Cards

A Liberal

I am glad that I live in a free and democratic society where everybody can do what he or she wants as long as it does not hurt others. In our society, you may decide to smoke, drink alcohol, use drugs or watch pornographic movies. It is ok to get married and have five children, but it is also accepted if you do not have a steady relationship or if you are gay or lesbian. It is entirely up to you how you spend your life. I wouldn't want to live in a different society. I value freedom most. I don't think too much freedom is confusing, but gives you the possibility to live your life as you want to.

A Fundamentalist

Young people need a firm belief and a reliable set of values by which to live their lives. Religion can offer them that. The problem of our society is that there are no longer any binding rules. So many people are confused about what to do. Nobody tells them whether it is ok to have sex before marriage, to smoke, gamble, drink alcohol, use drugs, what clothes to wear, etc. As a consequence, many young people do not really know what to do with their lives. They are experimenting with all sorts of cults and superstitions, having series of different relationships, do not value their freedom anymore and only see their own private pleasure. In the end many of them are left in ruins. Also peer pressure is a strong force. Since nobody tells them what to do, they end up doing what their classmates do without really thinking about it or being convinced of it. That is why we need to offer young people values and strict rules for their lives. That is what they really want – guidelines. It is the duty of religion to provide those guidelines.

Someone in-between

While I believe that freedom is an extremely important goal, I still think there should be certain rules in our society which we as teachers or parents should instill into our young people. Whereas I do not think we should be overly moralistic about certain issues, I believe we should still set a good example to our children by telling them that you may drink or smoke, but should not do so excessively because it ruins your health. And while you may have more than one partner in your life – because unfortunately relationships that were meant to last sometimes don't – we should not encourage them to sleep around and have sex with various partners without really being committed to them, because it does not foster real trust and understanding, but remains hollow and without emotional depth. I am glad that I live in the West, where I can decide freely what I want to do and nobody really restricts my private life; at the same time, I also see that many people, especially young people and teenagers, have problems with this lack of values and are looking for direction. We as teachers and parents have the responsibility to offer them goalposts for their lives by setting an example. Usually teenagers demand a lot of freedom, but too much freedom can be confusing because you are thrown back on yourself, and it is you who has to take responsibility for your own actions. Having all the freedom in the world is not only an advantage, but it can also be a burden to have too much freedom and not enough direction.

Text

"What's happened?"

"I've just had the worst experience of my life."

As Bettina rubbed his head Parvez told her that the previous evening[1], as he and his son had studied the menu, the waiter, whom Parvez knew, brought him his usual whisky-and-water. Parvez was so nervous he had even prepared a question. He was going to ask Ali if he was worried about his imminent[2] exams. But first he loosened his tie[3], crunched[4] a poppadum[5], and took a long drink.

Before Parvez could speak, Ali made a face[6].

"Don't you know it's wrong to drink alcohol?" he had said.

"He spoke to me very harshly[7]," Parvez said to Bettina.

"I was about to castigate[8] the boy for being insolent[9], but I managed to control myself."

Parvez had explained patiently[10] that for years he had worked more than ten hours a day, had few enjoyments or hobbies, and never gone on holiday. Surely it wasn't a crime to have a drink when he wanted one?

"But it is forbidden," the boy said.

Parvez shrugged[11]. "I know."

"And so is gambling, isn't it?"

"Yes. But surely we are only human?"

Each time Parvez took a drink, the boy winced[12], or made some kind of fastidious[13] face. This made Parvez drink more quickly. The waiter, wanting to please his friend, brought another glass of whisky. Parvez knew he was getting drunk, but he couldn't stop himself. Ali had a horrible look, full of disgus[14] and censure[15]. It was as if he hated his father.

Halfway through the meal, Parvez suddenly lost his temper[16] and threw a plate on the floor. He felt like ripping[17] the cloth from the table, but the waiters and other customers were staring at him. Yet he wouldn't stand for [18]his own son's telling him the difference between right and wrong. He knew he wasn't a bad man. He had a conscience[19]. There were a few things of which he was ashamed, but on the whole [20]he had lived a decent life.

---

[1]   the previous evening: the evening before
[2]   imminent: soon to take place
[3]   tie: Krawatte
[4]   to crunch: to crush s.th.noisily between your teeth when eating
[5]   poppadum (Hindi): a thin round crisp Indian bread, fried or roasted and often served with curry
[6]   to make a face: to produce an expression on your face to show you are angry or upset about s.th.
[7]   harshly: severely, unkindly
[8]   to castigate (formal): to criticizes.s.o. severely
[9]   insolent:very rude and showing no respect
[10] patiently: geduldig
[11] to shrug: die Achslen zucken
[12] to wince: to suddenly change the expression on your face as a reaction to s.th.painful or upsetting
[13] fastidious: showing that you are very sensitive, especially in matters that have to do with taste or correct manners
[14] disgust: extremely strong feeling of dislike because s.th. is very unpleasant
[15] censure: severe disapproval, strong criticism
[16] to lose your temper: to become uncontrollably angry
[17] to rip: to pull or tear violently
[18] to not stand for s.th.: to not accept, to not tolerate s.th.
[19] conscience: Gewissen
[20] on the whole: in general, for the most part

"When have I had time to be wicked[21]?" he asked Ali. In a low, monotonous voice, the boy explained that Parvez had not, in fact, lived a good life. He had broken countless[22] rules of the Koran.

"For instance?" Parvez demanded.

Ali didn't need to think. As if he had been waiting for this moment, he asked his father if he didn't relish[23] pork pies[24]?

"Well." Parvez couldn't deny[25] that he loved crispy[26] bacon[27] smothered[28] with mushrooms[29] and mustard[30] and sandwiched between slices of fried [31]bread. In fact, he ate this for breakfast every morning.

Ali then reminded Parvez that he had ordered his wife to cook pork sausages, saying to her, "You're not in the village [32]now. This is England. We have to fit in[33]." Parvez was so annoyed and perplexed[34] by this attack that he called for more drink.

"The problem is this," the boy said. He leaned across the table. For the first time that night, his eyes were alive. "You are too implicated in [35]Western civilisation."

Parvez burped[36]; he thought he was going to choke[37]. "Implicated!" he said. "But we live here!"

"The Western materialists hate us," Ali said. "Papa, how can you love something which hates you?"

"What is the answer, then," Parvez said miserably[38], "according to you[39]?"

Ali didn't need to think. He addressed[40] his father fluently[41], as if Parvez were a rowdy[42] crowd which had to be quelled[43] or convinced. The law of Islam would rule the world; the skin of the infidel[44] would burn off [45]again and again; the Jews and Christers[46] would be routed[47]. The West was a sink [48]of hypocrites[49], adulterers[50], homosexuals, drug users and prostitutes.

---

[21] wicked: morally bad in the way you behave
[22] countless: too many to be counted
[23] to relish: here: to get great pleasure from eating s.th.
[24] pork pie: Pastete mit Schweinefleisch
[25] to deny: to refuse to admit (leugnen)
[26] crispy: pleasantly hard and dry (knusprig)
[27] bacon: Speck
[28] smothered: here: completely covered with a large amount of s.th.
[29] mushroom: Champignon
[30] mustard: Senf
[31] to fry, fried, fried: to cook in fat in a pan
[32] in the village: i.e. in the village in Pakistan
[33] to fit in: here: to make sure that you are accepted by others
[34] perplexed: confused or worried because you don't understand .th.
[35] to be implicated in s.th.: to be involved in a crime or s.th. bad
[36] to burp (informal): rülpsen
[37] to choke: to be unable to breathe because you cannot get enough air
[38] miserably: in a way that shows you are very unhappy
[39] according to you: as you see it
[40] to address s.o. (formal): to speak directly to s.o.
[41] fluently: smoothly and skillfully without any pauses
[42] rowdy: noisy and likely to start a fight
[43] to quell: to stop (the) violent (e.g. of a crowd) behaviour
[44] infidel: here: a person who rejects Islam,. a non-believer
[45] to burn off: to burn and fall off
[46] Christer (slang): a Christian, especially one who is very religious
[47] to route: to defeat and cause to flee in confusion
[48] sink: cesspool (Sündenpfuhl)
[49] hypocrite: a person who pretends to have high moral standards (Heuchler)
[50] adulterer: s.o. who is married and has sex with s.o. that is not his/her wife or husband

While Ali talked, Parvez looked out the window as if to check that they were still in London. "My people have taken enough. If the persecution[51] doesn't stop, there will be *jihad*[52]. I, and millions of others, will gladly give our lives for the cause[53]."

"But why, why?" Parvez said.

"For us, the reward[54] will be in Paradise[55]."

"Paradise!"

Finally, as Parvez's eyes filled with tears, the boy urged[56] him to mend his ways[57].

"But how would that be possible?" Parvez asked.

"Pray[58]," urged Ali. "Pray beside me."

Parvez paid the bill and ushered his boy out [59]of there as soon as he was able. He couldn't take [60]any more. Ali sounded as if he'd swallowed [61]someone else's voice.

On the way home, the boy sat in the back of the taxi, as if he were a customer. "What has made you like this?" Parvez asked him, afraid that somehow he was to blame for all this. "Is there a particular[62] event which has influenced you?"

"Living in this country."

"But I love England," Perez said, watching his boy in the rear view mirror[63]. "They let you do almost anything here."

"That is the problem," Ali replied.

---

[51] persecution: treating people cruelly because of their relgious or political beliefs (Verfolgung)

[52] jihad (Arabic): a holy war against those who do not believe in Islam

[53] the cause: an idea or movement people are willing to fight for

[54] reward: s.th. you get for doing s.th. good

[55] Paradise: this belief is used, for example, by extreme Muslims to encourage young people to be suicide bombers,cf. Koran:Surah 47:4-5, which speaks of suicide when killing non-believers as way to get to Paradise

[56] to urge s.o. to do s.th.: to strongly suggest that s.o. should do s.th.

[57] to mend your ways: to stop behaving badly, to reform

[58] to pray: beten

[59] to usher s.o. out: to show s.o. the way out or to lead s.o. out

[60] to not take s.th. any more: to not be able to stand st.h. any more

[61] to swallow: to make food or drink go down your throat and into your stomach

[62] particular: certain

[63] rear view mirror: a mirror inside a car that lets the driver see the area behind the car

Tasks

1. Contrast Ali's with Parvez's attitude towards the Western world. You may go beyond the excerpt. (5 credits) (100–120 words)

2. Ali has not always been the way he is described in the excerpt. Describe the changes he has gone through prior to the passage above and explain what has precipitated his transformation. (5 credits) (100–120 words)

3. Characterize the father – son relationship in the chosen passage. Who has the upper hand in the conversation? You may go beyond the excerpt. (5 credits) (100–120 words)

II. Analysis (10 credits)

Compare Qaisra Shahraz's "A Pair of Jeans" to Hanif Kureishi's "My Son the Fanatic". Pay special attention to the attitudes parents and children assume towards their native Muslim culture and the more liberal, Western society they live in. (200–300 words)

III. Compostion (10 credits)

At one point in the story Ali orders his wife to cook pork sausages for him, saying: "You're not in the village now. This is England. We have to fit in." Explain Parvez's remark with reference to the whole story. According to you, to what extent should immigrants adapt to the country they live in or maintain their native customs and beliefs? Refer to at least two other stories from this collection. (200–300 words)

Key

I. Comprehension (15 credits)

1. Contrast Ali's with Parvez's attitude towards the Western world. You may go beyond the excerpt. (5 credits) (100–120 words)

Ali, Parvez's son, follows the rules of the Koran to the letter. The Koran dictates his daily lifestyle – drinking alcohol, gambling and eating pork are not allowed. He prays five times a day, gives away all his possessions, breaks up with his English girlfriend, and no longer sees his Western friends.

Since the Koran is his only guideline in life he knows exactly what is right and what is wrong and lectures his father about it. He accuses the West of being decadent and opposes its allegedly common practice of hypocrisy, adultery, homosexuality, the use of drugs and prostitution.

Parvez, on the other hand, has come to appreciate Western values and lifestyle and is a perfect model of assimilation. He eats pork and drinks alcohol and enjoys the freedom the West offers him. He does not find fault with having an extra-marital relationship with Bettina, a prostitute, or prostitution itself.

2. Ali has not always been the way he is described in the excerpt. Describe the changes he has gone through prior to the passage above and explain what has precipitated his transformation. (5 credits) (100–120 words)

Prior to the passage above Ali was a typical untidy, materialistic Western teenager. He did not like to clean up his bedroom, but left heaps of clothes, books, cricket bats and video games on the floor. He had his own TV, a video-player and a stereo system in his bedroom and used to play the guitar. He had an English girlfriend and many friends.

With his sudden change he becomes neat and orderly and gives away his new books, computer disks, videotapes and fashionable clothes as well as his TV, his video-player and his stereo system and takes down all the pictures in his room. In addition, he has developed a sharp tongue. Moreover, he not only renounces material possessions but also breaks up with his girlfriend and no longer sees his former friends. After a while Parvez realizes that a return to fundamentalist Muslim faith is the reason for his son's transformation.

3. Characterize the father – son relationship in the chosen passage. Who has the upper hand in the conversation? You may go beyond the excerpt. (5 credits) (100–120 words)

It is the son who sets down the rules and tells his father what to do and not to do, who admonishes the father not to drink alcohol, not to gamble and not to eat pork. The father, on the other hand, is not in control of his actions and as soon as his son begins to confront him with his allegedly wrong behaviour, he withdraws from him and begins to drink more. During the course of the conversation the son gains more and more the upper hand. It is Ali who controls the conversation and directs its course, not Parvez. Thus the text is characterized by a role reversal. The son's mounting superiority is contrasted with the father's increasing inferiority. In the end Parvez's emotions are stronger than himself and he is swept away by them. The moment Parvez strikes his son, he becomes a weak person no longer able to control himself. In contrast, Ali seems to bear each blow with serenity, thereby maintaining a detached and superior position.

II. Analysis (10 credits)

Compare Qaisra Shahraz's "A Pair of Jeans" to Hanif Kureishi's "My Son the Fanatic". Pay special attention to the attitudes parents and children assume towards their native Muslim culture and the more liberal, Western society they live in. (200–300 words)

When comparing "A Pair of Jeans" to "My Son the Fanatic", it becomes obvious that first and second generation immigrants, or to put it another way, parents and children can assume completely different attitudes towards the values of their native Muslim culture and those of the Western society they live in.

In "A Pair of Jeans" the first generation of immigrants (Ayub, Begum and Fatima) stick more or less to traditional Muslim values – in this case modest clothing for women – and the second generation (Miriam) demand more freedom and tolerance – being able to wear Western dress. In Kureishi's story the roles of parents and children have been reversed. It is Ali, the son, who lives a very strict, fanatic religious life, praying five times a day, getting rid of everything that is connected with the West – his guitar, his CDs and, most shockingly, his English girlfriend – and who develops a missionary attitude and is convinced that there is only one truth, one way to live by, one religion that can save the world – Islam. He even speaks of jihad and says that Western civilization has to be eradicated. It is no wonder that this makes Parvez cry and feel as if he has lost his son. This leads to an open confrontation with his father, who has completely assimilated a Western lifestyle.

Whereas "A Pair of Jeans" lives up to the readers' expectations that children tend to be less conservative than their parents and often rebel against the traditional set of values their elders try to imbue them with, "My Son the Fanatic" thwarts our expectations by showing us that young people, in their search for values and guidelines for their life in a complicated world, can have much more traditional, albeit fundamentalist attitudes than their elders. At the same time this story gives us an insight into the psychological reasons why the fundamentalist Islamic revival around the globe attracts so many young Muslims who have grown up in the West.

III. Composition (10 credits)

At one point in the story Ali orders his wife to cook pork sausages for him, saying: "You're not in the village now. This is England. We have to fit in." Explain Parvez's remark with reference to the whole story. According to you, to what extent should immigrants adapt to the country they live in or maintain their native customs and beliefs? Refer to at least two other stories from this collection. (200–300 words)

By telling his wife to cook pork sausages Parvez opposes the values of the Koran and adapts to English society. For Parvez there seems to be no reason in sticking to his native culture once he has moved to England. He completely adapts to Western society and does not make any effort to uphold his customs and traditions against the predominantly Western culture.

From a sociological point of view there are different ways of dealing with immigration. On the one hand there is the idea of the melting pot (complete assimilation of the immigrants into the new society) and on the other hand the idea of the salad bowl (taking pride in and celebrating diverse cultural heritage within a multicultural society, thereby enriching its dominant culture). Whereas the concept of the melting pot allows, ideally, for cultures to mingle and enrich one another, the salad bowl keeps the cultures distinct.

Issues such as the question whether Muslim teachers should be allowed to wear headscarves in European public schools show that the question whether immigrants should adapt to the society they live in or be allowed to celebrate their religion and their culture is still an ongoing discussion.

In Somerset Maugham's "The Force of Circumstance" Doris and Guy export British culture (playing tennis, drinking gin slings) to the colonies, but at the same time time adapt to Malay society. This is especially true for Guy who wears Malay dress.

In Muriel Spark's "The Black Madonna" Lou and Raymond at first sight seem to welcome the two Jamaican workers Henry Pierce and Oxford St. John with open arms, but are shocked when Oxford St. John takes pride in being black.

Ngugi wa Thiong'o is one of the few authors in this collection who is of the opinion that cultures should not mix but be kept separate and that "those coated with the white man's clay" (i.e. those who have partly assimilated Western values into their tribal culture) are the worst – meaning the people living in a transitory zone between the two cultures. To him all the trouble stems from mixing the two. In his opinion the purity of native cultures has to be preserved.

In my opinion immigrants should be allowed to take pride in their cultural heritage and at the same time accept certain rules of their new country's society, the language for example, in order to ensure that they understand and thus can enjoy the same rights as the native population.